MW00340479

• CELEBRATING HOLIDAYS & FESTIVALS AROUND THE WORLD •

Independence Days

Betsy Richardson

MASON CREST

Mason Crest
450 Parkway Drive, Suite D Broomall, PA 19008
www.masoncrest.com

Printed in the United States of America
First printing
9 8 7 6 5 4 3 2 1

Series ISBN: 978-1-4222-4143-1
Hardcover ISBN: 978-1-4222-4148-6

Library of Congress Cataloging-in-Publication Data is available on file.

Developed and Produced by Print Matters Productions, Inc. (www.printmattersinc.com)
Cover and Interior Design by Lori S Malkin Design LLC

QR CODES DISCLAIMER: You may gain access to certain third-party content ("Third-Party Sites") by scanning and using the QR Codes that appear in this publication (the "QR Codes"). We do not operate or control in any respect any information, products or services on such Third-Party Sites linked to by us via the QR Codes included in this publication, and we assume no responsibility for any materials you may access using the QR Codes. Your use of the QR Codes may be subject to terms, limitations, or restrictions set forth in the applicable terms of use or otherwise established by the owners of the Third-Party Sites. Our linking to such Third-Party Sites via the QR Codes does not imply an endorsement or sponsorship of such Third-Party Sites, or the information, products or services offered on or through the Third-Party Sites, nor does it imply an endorsement or sponsorship of this publication by the owners of such Third-Party Sites.

• CELEBRATING HOLIDAYS & FESTIVALS AROUND THE WORLD •

KEY ICONS TO LOOK FOR:

 Words to understand: These words with their easy-to-understand definitions will increase the reader's understanding of the text while building vocabulary skills.

 Sidebars: This boxed material within the main text allows readers to build knowledge, gain insights, explore possibilities, and broaden their perspectives by weaving together additional information to provide realistic and holistic perspectives.

 Educational Videos: Readers can view videos by scanning our QR codes, providing them with additional educational content to supplement the text. Examples include news coverage, moments in history, speeches, iconic sports moments and much more!

 Text-dependent Questions: These questions send the reader back to the text for more careful attention to the evidence presented there.

 Research projects: Readers are pointed toward areas of further inquiry connected to each chapter. Suggestions are provided for projects that encourage deeper research and analysis.

 Series glossary of key terms: This back-of-the book glossary contains terminology used throughout this series. Words found here increase the reader's ability to read and comprehend higher-level books and articles in this field.

CONTENTS

INTRODUCTION

Celebrating Holidays & Festivals Around the World

Holidays mark time. They occupy a space outside of ordinary events and give shape and meaning to our everyday existence. They also remind us of the passage of time as we reflect on Christmases, Passovers, or Ramadans past. Throughout human history, nations and peoples have marked their calendars with special days to celebrate, commemorate, and memorialize. We set aside times to reflect on the past and future, to rest and renew physically and spiritually, and to simply have fun.

In English we call these extraordinary moments "holidays," a contraction of the term "holy day." Sometimes holidays are truly holy days–the Sabbath, Easter, or Eid al-Fitr, for example–but they can also be nonreligious occasions that serve political purposes, address the social needs of communities and individuals, or focus on regional customs and games.

This series explores the meanings and celebrations of holidays across religions and cultures around the world. It groups the holidays into volumes according to theme (such as *Lent, Yom Kippur & Days of Repentance*; *Thanksgiving & Other Festivals of the Harvest*; *Independence Days*; *Easter, Passover & Festivals of Hope*; *Ringing in the Western & Chinese New Year*; *Marking the Religious New Year*; *Carnival*; *Ramadan*; and *Halloween & Remembrances of the Dead*) or by their common human experience due to their closeness on the calendar (such as *Christmas & Hanukkah*). Each volume introduces readers to the origins, history, and common practices associated with the holidays before embarking on a worldwide tour that shows the regional variations and distinctive celebrations within specific countries. The reader will learn how these holidays started, what they mean to the people who celebrate them, and how different cultures celebrate them.

▲ Fourth of July fireworks illuminate the sky above the New York City skyline.

These volumes have an international focus, and thus readers will be able to learn about diversity both at home and throughout the world. We can learn a great deal about a people or nation by the holidays they celebrate. We can also learn from holidays how cultures and religions have interacted and mingled over time. We see in celebrations not just the past through tradition, but the principles and traits that people embrace and value today.

The Celebrating Holidays & Festivals Around the World series surveys this rich and varied festive terrain. Its 10 volumes show the distinct ways that people all over the world infuse ordinary life with meaning, purpose, or joy. The series cannot be all-inclusive or the last word on so vast a subject, but it offers a vital first step for those eager to learn more about the diverse, fascinating, and vibrant cultures of the world, through the festivities that give expression, order, and meaning to their lives.

Independence Days

Almost every country in the world has a national holiday that commemorates the date on which the country came into existence as a nation, or to mark an important event in the nation's history. This holiday may be called Independence Day, Constitution Day, Freedom Day, or some other name. Whatever it is called, it is generally a time for people to gather with friends and family, eat, drink, and express their national pride.

▲ The Bristol County Fife & Drum Corps marches in Bristol, Rhode Island's 231st July 4 parade. The town's parade is generally considered to be the oldest July 4 parade in the United States.

▲ Boy Scouts and Girl Scouts stand and salute the flag during the Pledge of Allegiance at an Independence Day ceremony held at Thomas Jefferson's home in Monticello, Charlottesville, Virginia.

[January, 1770]

The true Sons of Liberty

And Supporters of the Non-Importation

Agreement,

ARE determined to resent any the least
Insult or Menace offer'd to any one or
more of the several Committees ap-
pointed by the Body at Faneuil-Hall, and
chastise any one or more of them as they
deserve; and will also support the Printers
in any Thing the Committees shall desire
them to print.

AS a Warning to any one that shall
affront as aforesaid, upon sure Information given, one of these Advertise-
ments will be posted up at the Door
or Dwelling-House of the Offender.

Origins of Independence Days

ationhood is a relatively modern concept. It was only during the late 18th century that people in Europe and North America began forming themselves into nations. For that reason, national days and independence days are all fairly new holidays. With a few exceptions, the earliest national days arose in the late 1700s; the most recent date from events that occurred in the 1990s.

WORDS TO UNDERSTAND

Apartheid: The practice in South Africa between 1948 and 1994 of keeping blacks and whites strictly separated in most areas of life.

Diaspora: A scattering; the dispersal of the people from a nation or ethnic group to places other than their traditional homeland. Capitalized, it refers to the experience of the Jewish people.

Empire: A state that has its political center in one place but exercises control over a number of other states or populations.

Vanguard: The leaders of a movement or action.

◀ The Sons of Liberty was an underground organization created in the years before the American Revolution to protect the rights of colonists and oppose British taxation of the colonies.

▲ King George III, depicted here in a stained glass window in London's Westminster Abbey, was king during the American Revolution.

■ Monarchs, Empires, and Colonies

Before nations were formed, most people were ruled by monarchs. They were subjects of a king, queen, prince, or other leader who inherited his or her authority. Often, people thought of themselves as subjects of a monarch, rather than citizens of a country. They were sometimes patriotic, in the sense of believing themselves to hold a particular nationality, though not always. National boundaries changed regularly as the result of wars and treaties, so a person could go to sleep in one country or **empire** and wake up in another.

Monarchies throughout the world frequently expanded their territory by conquering neighboring lands. Often they would claim these lands as colonies. When many colonies were held by a monarch, they were then considered to be part of an empire.

During the European Age of Exploration, from the 1400s through the 1600s, Europeans–especially those from Portugal, Spain, Holland, England, and France–sailed the globe looking for new lands. When they arrived in a new place, they would often claim it for their mother countries. This is how most of Latin America ended up in the hands of the Spanish and the Portuguese, and North America in the hands of the Spanish, French, and English. France, Great Britain, and Belgium divided up most of Africa. England, France, and the Netherlands claimed much of Asia. The Ottoman Empire, based in Turkey, ended up with most of the Middle East and North Africa, as well as a chunk of southeastern Europe.

Many Europeans moved from their homelands to the new colonies. They built homes, plowed fields, and did their best to maintain their European way of life. They were not alone, though. People lived all over the world before European explorers arrived claiming land as their own. The process of colonization inevitably resulted in conflicts with the indigenous people.

Colonists took several approaches to communicating with indigenous peoples. They often converted, or tried to convert, them to Christianity; missionary priests and ministers were always in the **vanguard** of colonists, and they went right to work spreading their religion. Colonists also might cooperate with indigenous people, learning from them. For example, the Thanksgiving celebrations in North America today are a result of positive early interactions between Native Americans and early settlers, even if many North American chroniclers have romanticized these early meetings to elevate the colonists.

More often, however, these contacts caused conflict. Through force and treaty early Europeans, with the backing of their monarchs, took lands and livelihood from the indigenous people. The Europeans often forced them to work as slaves and denied them the rights due to citizens. Colonists relied on soldiers to keep the native people from rising up against them.

Many indigenous people died at the hands of the European colonists. Some were killed deliberately and others died of diseases, such as smallpox, contracted from the colonists.

As colonies grew and thrived, the colonists typically began to resent their distant rulers. European colonists felt that they had worked hard to create their own societies and disliked having to pay taxes to their colonial monarchs. As time went on, colonists also often stopped feeling any real loyalty to their former homelands. Many of the children and grandchildren of original colonists had never been to Europe and had no reason to think of it as home.

■ Revolution

Many modern nations were born from revolutions. Resentments against the distant monarchs would build over time until colonial leaders declared independence, fighting a war against the ruling country if necessary. Eventually the new nation formed its own government. Many independence days commemorate a particular moment in this revolutionary process.

The United States was one of the first countries to rebel against its European rulers. The American Revolution was partly the result of a philosophical movement called the Enlightenment and new ways of thinking that were popular in France and North America at that time. Political philosophers of the 1600s and 1700s, such as John Locke and Jean-Jacques Rousseau, emphasized the natural rights of each individual rather than the authority of the state. Leading citizens in North America and Europe read about these concepts and began to develop their own ideas about how nations should be organized. This new philosophy inspired the U.S. Declaration of Independence, the document that launched the American Revolution in 1776.

The French Revolution followed closely on the heels of the American Revolution, erupting in 1789. Although French leaders were clearly influenced by the American experience, French revolutionaries were rebelling against their local monarch, unlike the Americans, who had fought against a distant one. Many of the Spanish colonies in Latin America followed suit and had their own revolutions in the early 1800s.

▲ Members of the Brigade of the American Revolution, an organization of amateur historians dedicated to preserving 18th-century American history, reenact a battle.

The next big wave of revolutions occurred in the early 1900s. Between 1910 and 1923, the collapse of the Ottoman Empire and the end of World War I resulted in a number of new nations, particularly in Eastern Europe and Central Asia. Many Asian nations were colonized by Japan in the first half of the 1900s; they became independent after Japan's fall in World War II (1939–1945). Many African nations became independent in the 1960s. The Soviet Union dissolved in 1991, creating new nations throughout eastern Europe and Central Asia. South Africa established its Independence Day on the date when **apartheid** ended in 1994. (Apartheid was the South African system of racial segregation.)

Learn about the French Revolution.

RAISING NATIONAL SPIRIT

A person is a citizen of the nation in which he or she is born. Some people feel a strong national identity, which may endure even if they move away from their homeland. They may raise their children as devoted citizens of a land in which they have never set foot.

This sense of attachment to a nation is called patriotism. The word *patriotism* comes from the Latin word "patria," which means "fatherland." A person's nation is thus the land of his or her fathers, the land to which he or she naturally belongs.

How to Make a Patriotic Citizenry

National governments work hard to foster patriotism. It is in a nation's best interest to keep its citizens loyal and proud of their homeland. They are then willing to pay taxes and, when necessary, fight in its wars.

Some governments encourage citizens to be patriotic in these ways:

- Designing and flying a national flag in distinctive national colors
- Teaching schoolchildren to pledge allegiance to the flag
- Designating a song as the national anthem
- Erecting national monuments that pay tribute to war heroes
- Holding parades that display military power
- Observing national holidays such as veterans' days, memorial days, and national and independence days

Public school systems play a big part in creating a patriotic citizen body. In the United States, for example, many students start every school day by pledging allegiance to the American flag. Children all over the world pledge allegiance to their flags, march in patriotic parades on national days, and perform patriotic ceremonies and plays at their schools. It is often considered an honor to be chosen to participate in one of these events, which emphasizes the value of patriotism.

Foundation Myths and National Heroes

At the heart of almost every independence day or national day is a story about the nation's founding. Mexico, for example, celebrates its independence on the date that the leaders of a rebellion against the Spanish urged fellow Mexicans to fight for freedom. The United States celebrates its independence day on the date when the nation's founders adopted the Declaration of Independence.

The story of a nation's beginning is often called a foundation myth. That does not mean the story is a lie. It means that as the source of a people's sense of national identity, it is generally a glorified, and often simplified, version of the truth. The people of every nation want to think of themselves as brave, resourceful, and, above all, on the side of justice. They like to think that it was inevitable that

▲ Malaysian king Sultan Muhammad V is accompanied by the prime minister after inspecting the royal guard of honor at the Parliament House in Kuala Lumpur, Malaysia.

they vanquished their enemies and erected a civilization in a particular place. When they celebrate their nationhood, they affirm their sense of the heroic, dramatic, and righteous origins of their country.

No story of a nation's founding is complete without heroes. Most liberation struggles begin with a few people who fight hard to win independence for their countries. They might be war heroes, such as the first president of the United States, George Washington, or Napoleon Bonaparte, a general during the French Revolution who later became emperor; or political leaders, such as Indian nationalist and social reformer Mohandas K. Gandhi, or Nelson Mandela, a

NOT EVERYONE LIKES NATIONAL DAYS

Most nations formed by colonization have diverse populations that include the descendants of native inhabitants. These indigenous peoples often feel that their ancestors were wronged by colonists and that their interests are still not respected by the government today. It is not unusual for these groups to protest national days or independence days.

▲ Every free nation has its founding heroes. India honors nationalist and social reformer Mohandas K. Gandhi, who was instrumental in gaining the country's freedom from Britain.

leading opponent of apartheid in South Africa who was elected president after apartheid ended. National heroes who die during the struggle to create a nation are considered martyrs by their countries. National day celebrations usually include some commemoration of these heroes and heroines.

■ When to Celebrate a National Holiday

It is not always obvious what day should become a nation's special holiday. Even after people settle on a particular date to celebrate, it may take many years for the government to make the date an official holiday. In France, the first national celebration took place just one year after the storming of the Bastille, a medieval prison, on July 14, 1789. The nation did not regularly celebrate Bastille Day, however, until the Senate made it an official holiday in 1880. Even then, the Senate was not entirely certain that July 14 was the best date. It also considered August 4, which was the date on which feudalism, the practice of peasants being tied to the land of nobles, was abolished in France. The violent storming of the Bastille made a better story, so the government chose July 14.

 TEXT-DEPENDENT QUESTIONS

1: When was the European Age of Exploration?

2: Name a political philosopher of the 1600s and 1700s.

3: What is the Latin origin of the word *patriotism*, and what does it mean?

 RESEARCH PROJECTS

1: Research an explorer from the European Age of Exploration. Find out facts about his life, where he explored, and other noteworthy information. Write a brief biographical sketch of the figure.

2: Research the history of apartheid in South Africa, including challenges faced by different groups, movements for freedom and equality, notable figures, and eventual changes to the law. Write a summary of your findings.

Celebrating Independence Days

Almost every national day celebration features speeches by politicians. In most countries, the president or national leader will address the nation, commending those who sacrificed themselves to create the nation, celebrating the nation's accomplishments, and setting forth its hopes for the future. The leader may mention difficulties that the nation currently faces and suggest possible solutions. Above all, he or she will remind listeners that they should be proud of their country.

WORDS TO UNDERSTAND

Constitution: A document that describes the organization of a nation's or state's government.

Monarchy: A system of government in which a single monarch, such as a king or queen, serves as the head of the state.

Regiment: A unit of the army composed of several smaller units called battalions.

◀ Every country has a flag, displaying the nation's colors. Flags are flown as a sign of patriotism on independence days throughout the world.

In many countries, large numbers of people watch national day speeches on television or listen to them on the radio. They may also gather at the presidential palace, residence, or other official location where the speech is being given, cheering wildly when the speech is over.

■ Raising the National Flag

National Day and Independence Day celebrations often include a flag-raising ceremony that takes place at dawn on the morning of the holiday. Flags fly to signify control over territory, to identify troops overseas, and to demonstrate the national allegiance of schools and other public institutions. Citizens display flags at their homes to proclaim their patriotism.

Flags are usually designed in a nation's national colors. Particular colors are often associated with certain qualities. For example, in the American flag, the red stands for courage, the blue stands for justice, and the white stands for purity. The combination of red, white, and blue reminds Americans of their flag, even when the colors are not in the standard flag design.

Experience an animation of some flags of the world.

The designs on a flag also have meaning. The stars on the American flag, for example, represent the 50 states, and the 13 stripes represent the 13 original colonies. Israel's flag has a six-pointed star in its center, signifying that Israel is a Jewish state. Kenya's flag features a Masai shield and spears, a reminder of Kenya's indigenous culture. Japan's flag is white with a large red circle in the middle representing the rising Sun, while the flag of the Federated States of Micronesia features a blue field representing the Pacific Ocean with four stars standing for the four island groups that make up the nation. The flag of the Republic of Ireland has a vertical white stripe in the middle signifying a truce between the green on the left (the Gaelic) and the orange on the right (the supporters of William of Orange). The flag of Mexico, red, green, and white, is distinguished from the similar Italian flag by the coat of arms in the center. The coat of arms comes from an Aztec legend.

Strict rules govern the use and care of flags. For example, most American children learn that a flag should never touch the ground, that it should be taken down from the flagpole at night, and that it must be folded a particular way. Schools and summer camps often have flag ceremonies at the start and end of each day that further instill respect for the flag. The flag is raised in a formal way, and the children pledge allegiance to it.

National flags tend to fly in abundance during national days. Children in Mexico, for example, like to carry flags with them at national day celebrations. People also like to dress in their national colors for national day celebrations.

■ Military Parades

Parades feature in national day celebrations throughout the world. Many of these parades are military displays that show off the nation's might. Dressed in their best uniforms, troops march along the city streets awing observers with their precision and polished appearance. Tanks might follow along. Often the national air force will fly fighter planes over the parade, or perform a separate air show. A parachute demonstration team might also jump into the city's main square.

Children often participate in these military parades. Schools around the world drill their students in marching and carrying the national flag. It can be a great honor to march in a national day parade.

BATTLE OF THE BOYNE DAY

In Ireland, Battle of the Boyne Day, also known as Orangemen's Day (or Orange Day), celebrates the historic victory of the Protestant William of Orange (1650–1702; he became King William III of England, Scotland, and Ireland) over his father-in-law and Catholic King James I (1650–1702). King James II was the king of England and Scotland (where he was known as King James VII) and Ireland. However, his dictatorship and lack of regard for Protestant beliefs angered his subjects, and he was ousted from the throne by his nobles. Instead of his son James Francis Edward (1688–1766) succeeding to the throne, his Protestant daughter Mary (1662–94) and her husband, William of Orange, assumed power. This led to a series of wars between King James II and William of Orange, in which James II was defeated in the Battle of Boyne on July 12, 1690.

The purpose of these parades (aside from the fact that parades are fun) is to show how strong the nation is. The nation's people must pay taxes to maintain their army, and it is gratifying to see those troops in action.

▲ Regiments parade down the Champs Élysées during the Bastille Day military parade in Paris. Bastille Day commemorates the storming of the Bastille prison on July 14, 1789, which set off the French Revolution that toppled King Louis XVI and put an end to the monarchy.

■ National Anthems

The national anthem is performed at some point during most national day celebrations. Usually, the anthem recounts the nation's struggles in achieving nationhood. For example, the national anthem of the United States, "The Star-Spangled Banner," describes a battle at Fort McHenry in Baltimore, Maryland, during the War of 1812. Anthems may also rally citizens to fight for their country if it is threatened. The Mexican national anthem begins "Mexicans, at the cry of war, prepare the steel and the steed." Though the Canadian national anthem, "O Canada!" speaks of defending the "true north, strong and free," two verses dwell on the natural wonders of the country, as in the lines:

O Canada! Where pines and maples grow,
Great prairies spread, and lordly rivers flow.

How dear to us thy broad domain,
From east to western sea.

The "Star-Spangled Banner" was set to the tune of an old British drinking song. The tune is that of the "Anacreontic Song," a drinking song that was written in the 1760s. In the early 1800s many different lyrics were set to this tune. When Francis Scott Key wrote "The Star-Spangled Banner," a poem describing a battle during the War of 1812, his brother noticed that its words fit the tune of the "Anacreontic Song"; and thus the U.S. national anthem was born. It became the official anthem in 1931.

THE OLDEST NATIONAL ANTHEM

The oldest national anthem is the Dutch, "Het Wilhelmus," which dates to the late 1500s.

National songs became popular during the rise of nations in the 1800s; today nearly every nation has one. Some nations adopt anthems when they become nations, either passing a law or writing the anthem into the national **constitution**. In other cases, the anthem starts as a popular patriotic song and gradually becomes accepted as the official song of the nation.

While typical anthems, such as France's "La Marseillaise," glorify the fight for freedom, other anthems, such as Bhutan's, make no reference to conflict or war. Bhutan is a small Asian country located in the eastern end of the Himalayan mountains, sandwiched between India and China. The anthem's lyrics were set to the melody of a folk song. Because the folk song already had dance steps, the Bhutanese may have the only anthem with accompanying choreography.

■ Upholding Cultural Traditions

Nations around the world hold outdoor festivals to celebrate their national days. These festivals may include carnival games and rides, free concerts and performances, and multiple food stands.

Picnics and outdoor activities are popular during national day celebrations, especially in nations where these holidays fall in the summer. In some countries such as El Salvador the national day holiday is part of a longer break, during which people can make trips to the beach, to relatives' houses, or to foreign countries.

Many nations use Independence Day celebrations to remind people of their cultural traditions. Celebrations often feature performances of traditional music or dance. Sometimes people dress in old-fashioned costumes for the day. Vendors may sell traditional crafts, such as

▲ A member of a choir in traditional dress from Indonesia's South Sumatra performs at the Independence Day celebrations at the presidential palace in Jakarta.

weaving or pottery. For many nations, no national day celebration would be complete without fireworks. Pyrotechnic extravaganzas are common around the world.

■ Celebrating Abroad

Many people throughout the world live in countries that are not their own. They may be living abroad temporarily for school or work, or they may have emigrated permanently. In either case, many people have a strong sense of national identity and continue to observe their home country's independence day.

Some of these observances are very quiet; Americans working in Japan on July 4 may have a barbecue on their own and shoot off a few fireworks, but the larger community is not affected. When enough people from a particular nation live in the same area, however, they may hold very large celebrations. Gambians in England, for example, gather to celebrate Gambia's Independence Day in London. Latvians in the United States have a thriving cultural community; even though many Latvian-Americans have not set foot in their country in years and their children may never have been there, they keep their cultural traditions alive and gather every year to celebrate Latvia's independence. Jews throughout the world celebrate Israel's independence every year.

▲ Young people hold up colorful banners as they march down Fifth Avenue in New York City during the annual Salute to Israel Parade.

■ The Importance of National Holidays

National holidays are essential to maintaining patriotism. Most people take a day off from work or school. They see their nation's colors everywhere and might wear those colors themselves. They are reminded in countless ways of their identity as a people, and they are encouraged to feel proud of their common accomplishments. They eat, drink, parade, and set off fireworks. A nation is strengthened when its people come together to celebrate.

▲ **Norwegians wave the flag for the National Day parade and celebrations.**

TEXT-DEPENDENT QUESTIONS

1: What does the white stripe in the flag of the Republic of Ireland represent?

2: What is the name of the tune the "Star-Spangled Banner" is based on?

3: What is the name of the French national anthem?

RESEARCH PROJECTS

1: Select a flag from any country of your choosing not covered in this chapter. Research the origins and history of the flag, what it symbolizes, any special flag protocols for that particular country, and other facts. Write a brief report summarizing your findings. Bonus: include your own color illustration of the flag.

2: Select a national anthem from a country of your choosing. Find out about its lyrics, melody, history of composition, and other facts. Write a brief report summarizing your findings, including when and how it is used in the country today.

Celebrating in Africa

Many African nations are relatively new. During the late 1800s, European empires divided up almost the entire continent. France, the United Kingdom, Portugal, Germany, Belgium, Spain, and Italy all laid claim to particular territories. They exploited these lands for commercial purposes and oppressed the indigenous peoples. They also exploited the existing difference between ethnic groups to keep African people from organizing themselves to revolt and throw out the Europeans.

European rule often made it difficult for African people to improve their living conditions. Black Africans were not allowed to vote or be educated. Some were sold to slave traders and shipped overseas into slavery; others were forced to work for Europeans in Africa as virtual slaves. They derived no benefit from the riches their continent had to offer.

After suffering under colonial rule for nearly a century, during the 1950s and 1960s, almost all of the nations of Africa won independence, in most cases through

WORDS TO UNDERSTAND

Civil war: A war between two portions of a single country, nation, or state.

Genocide: The practice of deliberately and systematically killing an ethnic group.

Guerilla attack: War carried out by irregular or unofficial armies.

◀ **Women take part in a parade at Freedom Day celebrations in Pretoria, South Africa.**

▲ Onlookers admire the fireworks during the celebration of Algerian independence from France, which occupied Algeria for 132 years.

persistent protests and fighting. The Algerian War of Independence, for example, was a bloody struggle against French rule that lasted from 1954 to 1962 and claimed many lives. After Algeria became independent, other French colonies in Africa were inspired to petition for freedom. By 1961 nearly all the French territories in Africa had gained independence without violence.

■ Rai Music in Algeria

On July 3, 1962, after nearly 1 million people died in the Algerian War of Independence, Algeria became independent from France. Thus today Algeria celebrates Independence Day on July 5, the anniversary of the French entry into Algeria. On the eve of Independence Day are government-sponsored concerts by famous *rai* stars such as Khaled (b.1960), Cheb Mami (B. 1966), and Rachid Taha (b. 1958). *Rai* is a style of music that is unique to Algeria. It combines Arabic melodies, French words, and North African trance music. On July 5, musicians in traditional dress crisscross the streets of the capital, Algiers, reminding the people of their hard-earned freedom. Flag-raising ceremonies are also part of the day's festivities. Since July 5 is a national holiday, schools, banks, and government offices are closed.

■ Dahomey Becomes Benin

Benin, formerly known as Dahomey, became completely independent from France as the Republic of Dahomey on August 1, 1960, which became its independence day. On Independence Day huge celebrations are held, and traditional dance and music performances take place all over Benin. Independence Day celebrations are presided over by the president, the official host of the foreign dignitaries invited for the occasion. Celebrations include parades by the armed forces, patriotic speeches, and cultural programs.

■ Botswana Day in Botswana

Botswana's independence day, Botswana Day, is celebrated on September 30 in commemoration of Botswana's freedom from the United Kingdom in 1966. Every year the people of Botswana come together and celebrate their nation. Botswana's capital, Gaborone, plays host to the celebrations. The national anthem, "Fatshe La Rona" (which means "our country") is sung proudly and is an important part of the celebrations. All institutions, both public and private, remain closed for two days as a sign of respect.

■ Independence Day in Chad

Chad was a French colony for most of the 20th century. In 1946, France began allowing the people of Chad to govern themselves, but kept the main source of leadership in Paris, France's capital city. In 1958, the people of Chad voted to become independent from France. Full independence arrived on August 11, 1960, which became Chad's national holiday. Because heavy rains in August often marred the celebrations and festivities, the government shifted the observance to January and Chad's independence is now celebrated on January 11 instead of August 11. On Independence Day most Chadians participate in Independence Day parades and many kinds of cultural activities that always include dance and music.

■ Celebrating in the Democratic Republic of the Congo

In the Democratic Republic of the Congo, Independence Day, June 30 is also a Memorial Day for those who died in the struggle for the Congo's freedom from Belgium. Official speeches and military parades are highlights of the day. Soldiers march in parades in the major cities. Those who cannot attend parades in person watch them on television. Television stations also broadcast movies that portray the Congolese struggle against Belgium.

Congolese families and towns have their own Independence Day celebrations. Barbecues are common, since most people in the Democratic Republic of the Congo raise their own chickens and goats. They invite their neighbors and relatives to come share the feast with them. Many

▲ Soldiers march in front of government officials during a celebration of Congo's independence.

Congolese people also visit cemeteries on Independence Day. They clean the graves of their relatives and put flowers on them.

■ Revolution in Egypt

Egypt was under British control during the early 20th century. It became free from British rule on February 28, 1922. It celebrates its national day on July 23, Revolution Day. This holiday commemorates the start of the Egyptian Revolution of 1952, a military coup that ended Egypt's monarchy and led to a republic. Egyptians celebrate Revolution Day with parades in the city streets. Homes, government offices, and buildings are adorned with bright lights. Grand feasts are part of the celebration and always include special sweets.

■ Town Festivals in Gambia

The Gambia became independent from Great Britain on February 18, 1965, a date now celebrated throughout the country. A national holiday, it is a day of great pride for Gambians. The annual Independence Day celebrations take place at the National Stadium in Bakau, near the capital city of Banjur. The president addresses the nation from the state house. Women dress in white turbans and caftans (ankle-length garments with long sleeves), some decorated with tie-dyed sunbursts. People throughout the country perform local dances wearing traditional costumes, such as long wrapped skirts or bushy robes made of reeds, sometimes carrying spears. Young men compete in wrestling matches.

In the Gambia, people do not eat much meat. On festive occasions such as Independence Day, however, they serve several meat dishes to mark the special day. Cooks serve up feasts of traditional foods such as *base nyebe* (a meat stew), *domadah* (meat stewed with groundnuts, served over rice), *benachin* (rice cooked with meat and vegetables), meat and fish served with cassava, and *chura gerteh* (a sweet rice and yogurt porridge).

■ Independence Day in Mali

Mali celebrates its independence on September 22. During the 20th century, Mali was part of a French colony called French Sudan. It supplied labor for French economic interests. Mali remained part of French West Africa until 1958, when it became part of the Soudan Federation. The Federation also included Senegal, Dahomey (today's Benin), and Upper Volta (now Burkina Faso). Dahomey and Upper Volta withdrew from the Sudan Federation in 1959,

Watch as Malians celebrate their Independence Day.

and the surviving union between Senegal and Mali (known as the Soudan Federation) ended when Senegal withdrew in August 1960. On September 8, 1960, Mali declared its independence. The president presides over Independence Day celebrations in Mali. In addition to parades of the country's armed forces and patriotic speeches, the day is celebrated with cultural festivals that include traditional dance and music performances.

■ Eating Goat in Mauritania

Mauritanians celebrate Independence Day on November 28, commemorating November 28, 1960, when the Republic of Mauritania was granted independence by its French rulers. To celebrate, Mauritanians eat festive meals that may include whole roasted goats or lambs stuffed with rice. Sometimes they eat camel. The main events include performances of traditional Arab music and processions lit by torchlight. All government offices and public and private institutions are closed on November 28.

■ Wearing Caftans and Djellabas in Morocco

Morocco declared itself free of French rule on November 18, 1956, after King Mohammed V returned from exile in Madagascar. Since that time, November 18 has been a major holiday in Morocco.

DRINK OF CHOICE IN NORTH AFRICA

Alcohol plays little or no role in most North African national day celebrations. Most of the people living in this region are Muslims and never drink alcohol. Mint tea is a much more common drink.

The day is celebrated with civic ceremonies such as flag-raisings, military parades, and public speeches. It is a public holiday on which government offices and schools are closed. Many Moroccans take the day off from work. People crowd the streets and markets, eating and drinking and greeting their friends. If the king makes an appearance, people jam the streets, hoping to catch a glimpse of him. To dress up, many Morrocan women wear long loose gowns called caftans. Men may wear robes called djellabas. Children tend to dress in Western clothing, such as shorts or pants, shirts, and dresses.

■ Somber Independence in Rwanda

Rwanda was a Belgian colony for most of the 20th century. In the 1950s Rwanda's indigenous leaders began agitating for independence, and on July 1, 1962, the country became an independent republic, free of Belgian control. Years of ethnic violence followed, as Rwanda's two main ethnic groups, the Hutu and the Tutsi, vied for control of the country. The situation degenerated into a full-fledged **civil war** in 1993. Thousands of people were killed in a **genocide**, or the deliberate killing of an ethnic, political, or cultural group, as Hutu tried to eliminate Tutsi from the country. Though the war ended in 1994 and the government is working to overcome the aftereffects of war and genocide, the Rwandan people have little enthusiasm for Independence Day celebrations.

However, on April 7 National Mourning Day, also known as Democracy Day and Genocide Remembrance Day is observed. On this day thousands of Rwandans gather in the national stadium in the capital of Kigali to remember the 800,000 Rwandans who died in the genocide of 1994. The ceremony begins by singing the national anthem and then observing three minutes of silence. The president lights a torch and places garlands on 20 coffins (obtained from digging up mass graves). Most offices and shops are closed on this day.

■ Freedom Day in South Africa

Every April 27 South Africa celebrates Freedom Day, commemorating the first nonracial and nondiscriminatory democratic elections, which were held in 1994, after the end of apartheid. South Africa spent several centuries under the control of white people of European descent. Through much of the 20th century South Africa was governed according to the rules of apartheid, in which blacks were systematically separated from whites and denied equal rights or opportunities. In 1912 native South Africans organized the African National Congress, which led the fight to improve conditions for blacks, defying the apartheid laws.

During the 1970s and 1980s violence escalated as black South Africans fought with increasing intensity for equal rights, especially the right to vote. Finally in the early 1990s the South African government began negotiating with the African National Congress to end apartheid.

▲ The granddaughter of Nelson Mandela, the first president of post-Apartheid South Africa addressed the crowd at a Freedom Day rally in Pretoria, South Africa.

The country adopted a new constitution in 1993, which came into effect on April 27, 1994. That day millions of South Africans voted in the first race-neutral election, electing Nelson Mandela as the nation's new president. April 27 became South Africa's Freedom Day, commemorating the first election held after the end of apartheid.

South Africa's government holds the national Freedom Day celebration in a different city each year. Typically, the president delivers a speech, and the South African National Defense Force performs an aeronautical display. All across the country, cities and towns hold their own festive Freedom Day celebrations. Communities put on parades with marching bands and drum groups, acrobatics displays, and performances of traditional dancing and singing. Most cities hold daylong concerts showcasing local talent. One of the most popular styles of music is called *isicathamiya* or *mubube*, an a cappella singing style, which means it has no instrumental accompaniment. This style originated with the Zulus, an indigenous people of South Africa, and black South Africans kept this tradition alive through the days of apartheid. Today *isicathamiya* groups participate in competitions to see who can make the best music. One of the best-known South African singing groups is Ladysmith Black Mambazo, which collaborated with American singer-songwriter Paul Simon on his album *Graceland*.

■ Independence Day in Tunisia

Tunisia's Independence Day, March 20, commemorates its independence from France in 1956. In 1878, France and the United Kingdom had decided that Tunisia would be a French protectorate if the British could in return control the Mediterranean island of Cyprus. Tunisians fought for their independence throughout the 20th century under the leadership of Habib Bourguiba, with supporters of independence launching **guerilla attacks** against their French rulers. Bourguiba intensified attacks on French troops and led widespread demonstrations against the colonial power. After the start of the Algerian War of Independence, France released Tunisia from its rule and Tunisia became independent on March 20, 1956. On Independence Day Tunisians pay homage to those who laid down their lives for the nation and its independence. Official speeches and parades by the armed forces are an integral part of the celebrations.

■ Rhodesia Becomes Zimbabwe

British explorers and missionaries arrived as early as 1850 in the region that was to become British-controlled Rhodesia. The European settlers voted to become a self-governing British colony in 1923, and the government excluded native Africans from voting, from ownership of the best farmland, and from most professions and skilled trades. Around 1965, under the leadership of Prime Minister Ian Smith, Rhodesia expressed its desire to break from British control, which Britain would agree to only under conditions found unacceptable by the Rhodesian government. In 1968 Rhodesia proclaimed itself a republic. Britain then complained to the United Nations, which imposed sanctions against Rhodesia. Meanwhile worsening race relations and guerilla attacks led many European farmers to abandon their lands. In March 1978, an agreement was signed to transfer power to the native Africans with Smith retaining the post of prime minister. The European ministry was forced to hold free and open elections. On April 18, 1980, Rhodesia became Zimbabwe, with Robert Mugabe as prime minister. Mugabe later became president in 1990. On April 18, all government offices, commercial establishments, and educational institutions remain closed in Zimbabwe. The national flag is unfurled at official Independence Day functions followed by parades.

TEXT-DEPENDENT QUESTIONS

1: What were the years of the Algerian War of Independence?

2: What country was formerly known as Dahomey?

3: When is Tunisia's Independence Day?

RESEARCH PROJECTS

1: Research one of the Algerian *rai* music stars mentioned in this chapter, including when they were born, how they got interested in music, and some of their noteworthy songs or albums. Write a brief biographical sketch of the figure. Bonus: listen to some of their songs online and include your own description of the music.

2: Research the state of Rwanda today, including how the country has recovered from the tragic period of civil war in the 1990s, economic or political advances, and challenges still to be faced. Write a brief profile incorporating your findings.

Celebrating in Asia

A sia is home to some of the world's oldest civilizations. China has existed as a political **entity** for thousands of years. Japan, Korea, and India also have long histories. During the rise of European nations during the 1700s and 1800s, much of Asia was colonized by Europeans. The British claimed India, the French took Southeast Asia, the Dutch laid claim to Indonesia, and the Spanish the Philippines. During the 20th century, Japan occupied Korea and other parts of Asia.

By the end of World War II in 1945, most of these colonies had been freed and new nations formed. China and other nations overthrew their monarchies and created new forms of government. This history has resulted in a variety of types of national days.

National day festivities are popular throughout Asia. People eat, drink, wear national colors, and march in parades. Above all, there are fireworks, which are an art form in much of Asia.

WORDS TO UNDERSTAND

Encroachment: An intrusion of one territory into another.
Entity: Something that has a distinct existence.
Innovative: Something that is new or inventive.

◀ A child waves a flag at an official ceremony in Hong Kong marking the anniversary of the founding of the People's Republic of China.

■ Struggles for Independence in Bhutan

Bhutan has struggled against **encroachment** from China. In 2005, Chinese troops entered Bhutan, supposedly because environmental conditions in the Himalaya Mountains forced them to cross the border. Soon afterward, the Chinese began building roads and bridges within Bhutanese territory. When the Bhutanese foreign minister objected, the Chinese responded that the border was "in dispute." In 2007, when the Bhutanese signed a new Treaty of Friendship with India, they carefully included a new phrase in the preamble, which reads ". . . reaffirming their respect for each other's independence, sovereignty, and territorial integrity." Clearly, the Bhutanese no longer take their independence for granted.

■ National Day in China

China celebrates its National Day on October 1. This marks the date in 1949 on which Mao Zedong founded the People's Republic of China (ROC) in a ceremony in Beijing's Tiananmen Square. Today Tiananmen Square is still a major center of National Day festivities. Crowds gather in Tiananmen Square in the morning to watch the national flag being raised and army troops assemble in the square to be reviewed by national leaders. The streets of Beijing are illuminated with white and colored lights. Festival organizers decorate the streets and squares of China's cities with red flags and banners and display portraits of China's most famous leaders.

Though in the past National Day celebrations were quite militaristic and featured military parades in city squares, today's Chinese people are more interested in entertainment. During the day many people attend parties in parks, followed by special television programs in the evening. Many cities sponsor large festivals, with food stands, games, and other entertainment. Dancers and musicians perform contemporary music and dances as well as traditional Chinese dances such as the Lion Dance. Chinese cities have also been known to import foreign performers such as Brazilian samba dancers. In addition, many Chinese people like to go to amusement parks. The famous National Day Cup horse races in Hong Kong are also featured during National Day.

A WEEK OF INDEPENDENCE

Most Chinese businesses and schools close for a week following October 1. Chinese people use this opportunity to travel. Tourist sites such as the Great Wall of China are mobbed during this week.

The Chinese take their fireworks seriously. Every town and city in China sponsors extravagant fireworks displays to celebrate National Day. The 23-minute Independence Day display in Hong Kong in 2007 cost about HK$3 million (Hong Kong dollars), which is about U.S.$380,000. Usually businesses and civic associations will pay most of the bill. The fireworks artists try to outdo themselves with **innovative** explosions. The 2007 Hong Kong display featured fireworks forming the numerals "08" to signify the 2008 Beijing Olympics and the numerals "10" to mark that Hong Kong had returned to China 10 years earlier. In 2008 the fireworks display and other National Day festivities attracted more visitors than in previous years, perhaps due to the worldwide attention received by the Beijing Olympics.

▲ Fireworks explode over Victoria Harbor to celebrate China's National Day in Hong Kong.

■ Independence from the British Celebrated in India

India celebrates Independence Day on August 15, the day India became independent from the United Kingdom. India was a British colony for more than 200 years. Led by freedom fighters such as Mohandas Gandhi and Jawaharlal Nehru, Indian activists spent many years in the early 20th century working to free India from British domination. Two years after the end of World War II, the British granted India its independence. At the stroke of midnight of August 14, 1947, the first prime minister of India, Jawaharlal Nehru, gave a speech declaring India's independence from Britain. He then raised the nation's new flag at New Delhi's Red Fort, a fortress constructed in 1639.

▲ The Red Fort, pictured here, was where India's first prime minister, Jawaharlal Nehru, declared India's independence and raised the country's new flag.

August 15 is now a national holiday in India called Swatantrata Diwas. Schools and businesses close and flag-raising ceremonies are held throughout the country, the largest in New Delhi, where India's prime minister still raises the flag at the Red Fort. The prime minister also gives a televised speech praising the people who fought for India's independence and reporting on the nation's progress. Schools hold their own flag-raising ceremonies. Once the flags are all waving in the breeze, Indians gather with their friends and families to celebrate. People may go on picnics or have parties at their homes. Various clubs and organizations hold Independence Day Festivals with games and performances that highlight India's independence.

Children all over India fly kites on Independence Day. They go out to parks or climb up on rooftops and spend hours flying kites made in India's national colors of green, white, and saffron yellow, many of them decorated with the faces of political leaders such as Indian prime minister Indira Gandhi (1917–1984). Kids gather in groups and feed out more and more string as their kites soar higher and higher. Some children like to fight with their kites, trying to use their kite string to cut the strings of kites that encroach into their airspace. Good kite fighters consider their sport an art form; they use heavy kite string and big kites that are easy to control in rapid sweeping motions, and they consider fingers bruised from controlling the powerful kites to be a badge of kite-fighting honor. This tradition is said to date back to 1947, when the sky filled with Indian kites as soon as the British flag was lowered for the last time.

■ Multi-Day Celebration in Indonesia

Indonesia's Independence Day is August 17 commemorating the day it won its freedom from centuries of Dutch rule in 1945. Preparations for Independence Day start ahead of time when office buildings, shopping malls, and the fences around government buildings are festooned with red and white banners, the colors of Indonesia's flag. The capital city, Jakarta, decorates its main streets with red and white lights. Everywhere banners proclaim "Dirgahayu Ri," or "Long Live Indonesia."

For days before the holiday, newspaper and television commentators share their insights into the country's progress since independence. Schools hold contests to see which class can create the most patriotic decorations. Classes also compete in games and races. Citizens work together to clean up their communities, pulling weeds, repainting public areas, and cleaning drains. Some neighborhood associations require members to fly the Indonesian flag, with its two equal wide horizontal stripes, red above white, in front of their houses; in the past, people even repainted their homes so they would look nice for the holiday.

Government offices, banks, and schools close, though some businesses and restaurants do stay open. Towns and cities throughout the country hold celebrations with fireworks and food stands on the streets. Children walk through the streets waving Indonesian flags and wearing Indonesia's national colors. Musicians play patriotic concerts, which are broadcast on television throughout the nation. There are public ceremonies throughout the country, especially in the capital city of Jakarta. The president makes a speech and hoists the Indonesian flag at the National Palace. There is also a ceremonial gun salute. The massive military parade in Jakarta is one of the highlights of the day. High school students from throughout Indonesia are selected to march in this parade, executing intricate steps as they march past the president and the cabinet.

Neighborhoods hold less solemn celebrations. Children decorate their bikes, play games, and compete in foot races. One popular game is the *krupuk* eating contest. *Krupuk* are fried shrimp chips, a favorite Indonesian snack. Women compete with one another to see who can fry the biggest *krupuk* or cook other dishes such as *nasi tumpeng*, a traditional Indonesian dish of rice, coconut milk, fried chicken, salted fish, and other delicacies.

On their Independence Day, August 17, Indonesian children and adults love to play a game called *panjat pinang*, in which prizes are hung from the top of a greased Areca palm tree trunk. Children race to shimmy up the slippery trunk and claim the prizes. Everyone gets completely covered with mud, much to the amusement of spectators. The prizes are often well worth the effort— bicycles and television sets are typical. *Panjat pinang* is not a solitary sport, though; the best way to reach the top is through teamwork, with people standing on top of each other to reach the top of the pole. When a team succeeds in claiming the prizes, they may sell the items at an auction and share the money.

PAKISTAN'S FLAG

The flag of Pakistan has a vertical white band (symbolizing the role of religious minorities) on the hoist side. There is a large white crescent and a star in the remaining green portion of the flag; the crescent, star, and green color are traditional symbols of Islam.

■ Independence Day in Pakistan

Pakistan is one of the largest Muslim nations in the world. It was initially part of India, but due to irreconcilable conflicts between Muslims and Hindus, two separate nations were formed in 1947, the year that India achieved independence from British colonial rule. Celebrated on August 14, schools,

▲ Young men climb slippery tree trunks to get prizes during a popular game known as *panjat pinang* in Jakarta, the capital of Indonesia.

government offices, and businesses all close for Independence Day in Pakistan. To celebrate this occasion, there are meetings, rallies, and demonstrations celebrating the formation of Pakistan. The first people up and about on this day are the street cleaners paid by the government to get the roads clean. The government and military perform in parades in the morning. Then the army and Boy Scout troops march past the assembly building in the capital. The soldiers conclude the parades by firing a shotgun. After the parades are over, students assemble at their schools, which are decorated with national flags.

They perform national dances and give speeches about Pakistan's history. Afterward, everyone goes back home to eat sweets and relax with their friends and relatives.

■ Dodging Bombs in Colombo, Sri Lanka

Sri Lanka celebrates Independence Day on February 4, commemorating the day it became independent from the United Kingdom in 1948. It is officially celebrated by military parades, pageants, national games, and dances in various parts of the country.

In 2008, the government of Sri Lanka received warnings that rebel groups of Tamil Tigers would attempt to detonate bombs during the Independence Day celebrations. The government sealed off roads in the capital city of Colombo to allow parades to pass through and vendors to set up booths on the streets. Despite these precautions, a number of bombs exploded, killing 12 civilians and one soldier. The Tamil Tigers represent a minority ethnic group called the Tamils. They believe that they are unfairly dominated by the Sinhalese people, who make up 74 percent of Sri Lanka's population and control the government. The Tamil Tigers are fighting to create their own nation independent of the Sinhalese.

■ Double Ten in Taiwan

Taiwan has a complicated history. The island was controlled for centuries by imperial China and then colonized by the Japanese in 1895 before reverting to Chinese control in 1945. In 1949, the Chinese Communist Party won a civil war and established the People's Republic of China (ROC), controlling nearly all of mainland China but not Taiwan.

Taiwan's National Day commemorates an important day in the history of the Republic of China, October 10, 1911, when a nationalist revolt began, the Wuchang Uprising, that eventually overthrew the Qing dynasty and created a republic. The holiday is called Double Ten because it is celebrated on the 10th day of the 10th month. Political and military displays are the focus of the holiday, with the celebrations centered in the presidential office

Experience a National Day parade in Taiwan.

building. Thousands of people travel from all over the country to watch a military parade and hear the president address the nation. The crowd sings the Republic's national anthem and enjoys a parade showcasing the many professions in Taiwan, folk dances and theatrical performances, and several hours of fireworks.

Not all Taiwanese like this national day, however. Officially, Taiwan is still part of China. Many Taiwanese believe that Taiwan should be an independent nation. A group of pro-independence agitators sometimes celebrate a Taiwanese Independence Day in Taipei, Taiwan's capital city. In the early 21st century, a group of activists assembled at the presidential office in Taipei to raise a flag for the "Republic of Taiwan" and sing *Taiwan the Green* (which members of the Taiwan independence movement have proposed as a future national anthem by the Republic of Taiwan). Several young people recited a declaration of Taiwan's independence. The group claimed that it was commemorating Taiwan's independence, dating the event back to the San Francisco Peace Treaty of 1951, in which Japan gave up its claim to Taiwan.

■ Independence Celebrations in Vietnam

Communist leader Ho Chi Minh declared Vietnam independent from the French on September 2, 1945. However, the Vietnamese Communist Party controlled only North Vietnam, and South Vietnam fought for its independence against the communist north. War raged in Vietnam for 30 years, costing millions of lives. In 1961 the United States joined the war between north and south, supporting South Vietnam's fight for independence, eventually committing large ground forces. Among the American people, opposition to the war grew steadily through the 1960s and early 1970s. In 1973, the U.S. military pulled out of Vietnam. By 1976, the South Vietnamese government had fallen, and the country was united under communist control.

Even after the fighting ended, Vietnam remained devastated for decades. During the 1990s Vietnam's economy and living conditions improved tremendously, but the nation is still quite poor. Today, Vietnamese people observe the anniversary of their nation's independence on September 2, which commemorates the date in 1945 on which the Vietnamese leader Ho Chi Minh declared

▲ Women from Vietnam's central highlands dance during the Independence Day celebrations in Hanoi.

Vietnam independent from France. Thousands of people gather in Vietnam's main square in Hanoi, Vietnam's capital, to listen to political speeches and watch a parade featuring young men and women in traditional costume waving flags and banners. Ho Chi Minh died in 1969, but his face lives on in Vietnamese Independence Day decorations. Although the Vietnamese flag (a red flag with a gold star at its center) is a popular decoration, pictures of Ho Chi Minh are also everywhere. Posters, banners, flags, and even baseball caps show images of his face. An evening fireworks display completes the celebration.

TEXT-DEPENDENT QUESTIONS

1: Who founded the People's Republic of China in 1949?

2: Who was Jawaharlal Nehru?

3: In what country is *panjat pinang* played?

RESEARCH PROJECTS

1: Research the life of Mohandas Gandhi, including his origins, early life, and growing involvement in civil rights causes. Compose a brief biographical sketch, including key moments in the struggle for Indian freedom and how he contributed to them.

2: Select one of the countries profiled in this chapter. Research foods native to that country that people might eat on their Independence Day or other festive celebration. Write brief descriptions of these dishes, including recipes if available.

Celebrating in Europe

Europe is home to some of the world's oldest nations. Most of Europe was dominated by monarchies and empires throughout the 18th century, and many areas were divided into small states called **principalities**. Italy, for example, was not a unified nation, but instead a collection of numerous small kingdoms.

This state of affairs began to change with the French Revolution in 1789, which ended the French monarchy. During the 1800s nations formed out of smaller principalities that unified with one another. For example, Germany created an empire that **encompassed** most of modern Germany, Poland, and Lithuania. The Austro-Hungarian Empire formed in 1867 in the region that is now home to Austria, Hungary, and other eastern European nations. The Russian Empire dominated Russia and the rest of eastern Europe, while the Ottoman Empire controlled most of southeast Europe.

WORDS TO UNDERSTAND

Encompass: To contain or surround.
Principality: A small state ruled by a monarch called a prince.
Rosette: A type of decoration resembling a rose.

◀ Fireworks explode over Madrid in celebration of Spanish independence.

All of these empires dissolved at the end of World War I (1914–1918), resulting in a number of new nations. Beginning in 1922, the Soviet Union took over much of the territory of the Russian Empire and held it during most of the 20th century, until it dissolved in 1991. With the end of the Soviet Union many new nations have formed in eastern Europe, amid much tension and some violence, especially in the former Yugoslavia. Brand new national days are celebrated across eastern Europe.

Several festivals in particular illustrate the development of European nations and the rise of national days. Bastille Day in France is the first of the European national days, dating back to the period of national revolutions in the late 1700s. Unity Day in Germany is a much more recent festival, celebrating Germany's reunion after years of being divided during the 20th century. All of the former Soviet Republics are still developing their national days, having only recently been allowed to form independent nations. Regardless of how they became nations, most European nations celebrate their national days with the festivities that often celebrate independence around the world: military parades, air shows, street festivals, and fireworks.

■ Getting One's Fill in Belgium

BELGIUM'S NATIONAL RAINSTORM

It often rains on Belgium's national day celebrations; this happens so frequently that it is something of a tradition for Belgians, who call it the "national rainstorm."

Belgium celebrates National Day on July 21, the date on which Belgium's first king, Leopold I, swore allegiance to the nation's constitution at the royal palace in Brussels (Belgium's capital) in 1831. It was after Belgium was separated from the Netherlands on October 4, 1830, that the Belgian National Congress asked Leopold to be the king. Leopold agreed, and the day he was crowned became the Belgian national holiday.

This independence day is a national holiday and government offices, schools, and businesses are closed. Belgians throughout the country celebrate by eating, drinking, and watching a parade featuring the royal family.

In Waterloo, the town sets up tents in front of the city hall. At this national day celebration, everyone eats and drinks huge amounts of food and Belgian beer. Musical groups perform and revelers fill a dance floor. Children play in nearby parks. Red Cross volunteers sit next to the beer tents, ready to render aid to anyone who gets sick or injured.

■ Bastille Day: La Fête de la Fédération in France

France was not only one of the first European nations to end its monarchy and become a modern republic, but it was also one of the first to celebrate a national holiday. France's national day, called Bastille Day and La Fête de la Fédération (Festival of the Federation), is celebrated on July 14. It commemorates the day in 1789 on which the French people stormed the Bastille, a prison in Paris. Some people consider this event the real start of the French Revolution.

At the time, France was ruled by King Louis XVI and his wife, Marie Antoinette. The country was suffering a major financial crisis, and the king had responded by raising taxes. In protest, the people formed a National Assembly and wrote a constitution for France. They also created a national guard, which wore **rosettes** of red, white, and blue, the colors of the French flag. This national guard started attacking the houses of nobles to prevent them from shutting down the National Assembly. On July 11, Louis XVI, in something of a panic, reorganized his cabinet. The people who supported the National Assembly interpreted this as a hostile sign and began to riot.

On July 14, a group of citizens invaded the Bastille. Although the Bastille held only seven prisoners, the people saw it as a symbol of tyranny. The rebels found a large quantity of gunpowder

▲ The Eiffel Tower is illuminated during the traditional Bastille Day fireworks display in Paris.

and some guns, which they seized for their own use. During the conflict, the citizens killed the royal guards. The king capitulated and withdrew his forces.

That August the people of France outlawed feudalism, the medieval form of social organization in which nobles controlled the labor of peasants. On August 26, the people of France proclaimed their Declaration of the Rights of Man and of the Citizen, which declared the natural rights to which all humans are entitled. (This document is similar to the U.S. Declaration of Independence.) France was on its way to transforming from a monarchy to a republic, though this process was to take many more years.

On July 14, 1790, the people of France held their first Fête de la Fédération to celebrate what they thought was the end of the French Revolution. Thousands of people assembled at the Champ de Mars, a large public park in Paris. The king swore to uphold the new constitution that created a constitutional monarchy. (A constitutional monarchy combines rule by a hereditary monarch, such as a king or queen, with a national constitution and a parliament that makes laws. This way the monarch does not have complete power over the government.) The people of Paris spent four days feasting, setting off fireworks, and drinking wine in celebration. However, as it turned out, the revolution was not over, and France spent several more years in chaos, as citizens arrested and killed a number of nobles, as well as the king and queen. France went through several governments over the next century starting with Napoleon Bonaparte, who became emperor in 1804. Under the emperor Napoleon, France became a major military power, enjoying a string of victories against other European nations before succumbing to the British and Prussians at Waterloo in 1815.

BICYCLING ON BASTILLE DAY

The Tour de France, the most famous bicycle race in the world, takes place over two weeks in July. Bastille Day falls on one day of the race every year. The French team always tries especially hard to win that day's race.

By 1870, however, France had once again created a republican form of government, known as the Third Republic. In 1878 the government decided to create a national day to honor the Republic, and chose July 14, when the people stormed the Bastille, as the most appropriate day. France's Assembly made the holiday official in 1880, and since then the French have celebrated Bastille Day with gusto.

One of the biggest events of Bastille Day is the military parade that passes down the Champs Élysées, the widest street in

Paris. The composition of the parade varies slightly from year to year. Sometimes visiting troops from other countries lead the parade. For example, in past

See highlights of Bastille Day celebrations in Paris.

parades, representatives from the states of the European Union have walked first. (The European Union is a political and economic union of 27 member states, mainly located in Europe.) If there are no guests, cadets from various military schools, such as the École Polytechnique start the parade. Next come French soldiers marching on foot, with members of the French Foreign Legion at the back of the line. They are followed by tanks, trucks, and the Paris Fire Brigade. The Patrouille Acrobatique de France, the aerobatic team from the French Air Force, flies over the city performing aerial stunts, accompanied by helicopters and airplanes from the French navy and air force.

■ Rebirth for Germany

Germany's national day is October 3, Unity Day. This day commemorates the anniversary of Germany's reunification in 1990. After World War II ended in 1945, Germany's was divided into two countries, West Germany and East Germany. West Germany was an independent western European nation, while East Germany was a socialist state created by the Soviet Union. Families were sometimes split apart by the division. A wall divided Germany's capital into West and East Berlin, and traveling between the two sides was not permitted. In 1989, with the Soviet Union collapsing, East Germany began permitting its citizens to travel to the West. Berliners began climbing over the wall and tearing it down piece by piece. Eventually the government dismantled the entire wall and made reunification official on October 3, 1990.

Unity Day is the only German holiday legislated by federal law. (Other public holidays in Germany are made by laws in the individual German states.) The German government had to choose between two dates for a national day: the date of reunification, or the date on which the Berlin Wall fell. As it happened, the choice was easy. The Berlin Wall came down on November 9, 1989, but November 9 is also the anniversary of the Kristallnacht, the night in 1938 when the Nazis, under the leadership of Germany's Chancellor Adolph Hitler, murdered nearly 100 Jews, arrested tens of thousands more, and destroyed thousands of synagogues and Jewish homes and businesses. Celebrating Germany's national holiday on that date seemed inappropriate, so the government chose October 3.

▲ Celebrations of the 25th anniversary of German reunification in 2015 included a laser light show in Frankfurt, Germany.

Most businesses and schools close for Unity Day. People take the day to travel, attend town festivals, and consume large quantities of traditional food and drink such as sausages and beer. The largest celebration in Germany is the Bürgerfest, or Citizens' Festival, which is held in a different city every year.

The Unity Day celebrations in Berlin in 2000, 10 years after Germany's reunification in 1990, were particularly dramatic. Hundreds of thousands of people gathered in the city streets near the Brandenburg Gate, the only gate left of the several through which one entered Berlin. They danced on the site of the former Berlin Wall, rejoicing in their freedom to move between East and West. Some people dressed up as Berlin buildings, including the Brandenburg Gate. Free concerts drew large crowds to the Reichstag parliament building.

■ Children's Parades in Norway

May 17 is Norway's Constitution Day. Norway celebrates this day with parades, not of soldiers but of children from all across the country. The children carry national flags–red with a blue cross outlined in white; the vertical part of the cross shifted to the hoist side–and school banners. School marching bands play patriotic songs. Thousands of people come out to watch the children marching; some spectators become so enthused that they end up joining the parades and march back to the schools with the children. The parade in Oslo, Norway's capital, is the nation's largest, featuring more than 100 schools. In this parade the children march past the royal palace, where the king and queen wave to them.

■ Former Soviet Republics

Many of the former Soviet Republics became independent twice in the 20th century. The first time was during or after the end of World War I, when the Russian, German, Astro-Hungarian, and Ottoman Empires collapsed. The Soviet Union retook most of these nations during the 1920s, 1930s, and 1940s. The same nations—known as the "Baltic states" for their bordering the Baltic Sea—once again became independent in 1990 or 1991, after the Soviet Union dissolved. These nations then faced a choice—whether to celebrate their first Independence Day or their second. Some chose to celebrate both.

For many nations that were part of the Soviet Union or the Eastern Bloc during the second half of the 20th century, independence days are still a work in progress. The nations lost much of their native culture under Soviet dominance. The Soviets did not allow people to practice their native customs and often insisted that they speak Russian instead of their native languages.

FESTIVITIES IN ARMENIA

Armenia has two independence days. One marks Armenia's liberation from the Soviet Union and formation of an independent republic on September 21, 1991. The other Independence Day commemorates the first time Armenia became independent in 1918. Armenia was under the control of the Ottoman Empire for 600 years before it became independent on May 28, 1918. Many Armenians consider this their first independence day.

Armenia's people put on a number of events to celebrate independence. Most Armenian churches hold special services. During the week preceding Independence Day the Ministry of Culture and Youth Affairs in the capital, Yerevan, shows films that have been made in Armenia since independence and holds art exhibits and youth concerts. On September 21, cities and towns hold celebrations all day long. In the morning, the celebrations open with a military parade in Republic Square as a display of the defense capability of the Armenian armed forces, featuring the latest arms and ammunitions acquired by the country. There is also a flag-raising ceremony and a speech made by the president, as well as cultural activities. Festivals with food stalls and games are held throughout Yerevan. In the evening, the government sponsors numerous fireworks displays throughout the country.

AMBIVALENCE IN LATVIA

Latvia first declared independence from Russia on November 18, 1918. After years of Soviet dominance, it once again became an independent nation on May 4, 1990. Latvia now celebrates both days, November 18 as National Day and May 4 as Independence Day.

Fireworks are a major part of the celebrations on November 18. Latvia does not yet have many traditions for celebrating Independence Day on May 4. The holiday has not existed for very long, and Latvians have mixed feelings about what would be appropriate. Many people dislike the idea of holding a military parade, largely because the May 4 declaration of independence stressed non-violence.

TWO INDEPENDENCE DAYS IN LITHUANIA

Like Latvia, Lithuania also has two Independence Days: February 16 and March 11. These days commemorate the two times during the 20th century that Lithuania declared its independence. Lithuania first declared itself an independent republic on February 16, 1918, from Imperial Russia. In June 1940, the Soviet Union invaded Lithuania and the other Baltic States and incorporated them into the Soviet Union. Lithuania declared independence again on March 11, 1990, becoming the first of the former Soviet republics to do so.

Lithuania celebrates February 16 with parades, speeches, patriotic songs, and other official events. In 2008, for example, the president of Lithuania used the day to meet with the presidents of Estonia, Latvia, and Poland to celebrate all three countries' independence from the Soviet Union. After the presidents attended a mass at Vilnius Cathedral, the Lithuanian armed forces staged a parade through Cathedral Square. That evening there was a gala party at the Lithuanian National Opera and Ballet Theatre and a concert in Cathedral Square. The people of Lithuania celebrated the day by watching the parade and then attending performances, parties, and concerts. In Lithuania, Independence Day is always an occasion to eat traditional delicacies such as potato dumplings called *cepelinai* (named after the type of airship called a zeppelin) and a beet soup called borscht, and to drink the famous Lithuanian beer.

On March 11, huge celebrations are held in different parts of Lithuania. In the capital city of Vilnius, the president presides over the celebrations. All those who lost their lives during Lithuania's quest for independence are remembered, and the achievements of the republic are also acknowledged on this day. Besides the official speeches, a cultural festival is organized that celebrates the rich cultural heritage of the country.

◀ Fireworks explode over the Dnieper River in Kiev, Ukraine to celebrate Independence Day.

INDEPENDENCE IN UKRAINE

On August 24, 1991, Ukraine became independent from the Soviet Union and was declared a sovereign state. This day is celebrated all over Ukraine with festivals, military parades, and performances by military orchestras. Most businesses close, but market vendors are open for business. Ukrainians enjoy going to these open-air markets where they can buy all sorts of items. Some stalls even sell cars! On Independence Day, some Ukrainian cities hold circuses for children. In the evening, most people go to watch fireworks. Teenagers and young adults then go out to parties to continue celebrating.

■ Independence Celebrated in Turkey

In Turkey, October 29 is Republic Day. This commemorates the date on which the Republic of Turkey was proclaimed the successor state to the Ottoman Empire in 1923. On this day government offices and schools close. Every city holds celebrations, but the largest is held in Istanbul. The nation's military puts on a parade that ends in a ceremony during which government officials give speeches. Students have the day off from school, but many of them use the day to participate in patriotic shows. People everywhere walk around carrying national flags and torches and singing nationalistic songs, both as part of organized parades and on their own. At night, the city governments sponsor fireworks displays.

▲ Britain's Queen Elizabeth II rides in a state coach on the way to the annual ceremony opening Parliament.

■ Singing Happy Birthday to the Queen in the United Kingdom

The closest thing the United Kingdom has to a national day is the king or queen's official birthday. Although the current monarch, Queen Elizabeth II, was born on April 21, her official birthday is celebrated on the first, second, or third Saturday in June. The monarch's official birthday has been celebrated in June since the time of King Edward VII (1901–1910). England is notoriously rainy, but June has some of the best weather of the year; King Edward hoped that holding the holiday in June would maximize his chances for a sunny Saturday.

The Queen's birthday is not a public holiday, which means that people who work on Saturdays still have to go to work. In London, the army performs the ceremony of Trooping the Colour, which in this case is called the Queen's Birthday Parade.

TEXT-DEPENDENT QUESTIONS

1: Who was Belgium's first king?

2: What is the name of the widest street in Paris?

3: Why does Armenia have two independence days?

RESEARCH PROJECTS

1: Research a city outside of France where Bastille Day is celebrated. Examples include New York, London, and Prague. Write a brief summary of how the holiday is celebrated in the city, including any special customs or events.

2: Research one of the Baltic states, including information about its history, economy, form of government, language, and arts and culture. Write an overview of this country that incorporates your findings. Be sure to include information on the state of the country today.

6

Celebrating in Latin America and the Caribbean

atin America was colonized by the Spanish and Portuguese during the 16th and 17th centuries. By the beginning of the 1800s, most Latin Americans of European descent were ready for independence. They had seen the United States and France spark revolutions and create new forms of government, and decided that they were ready to do the same thing.

The first Latin American nation to demand independence was Ecuador. On August 10, 1809, the leaders of the colonists in Quito, the capital city, called for independence from Spain. This event is known as the "Primer Grito de la Independencia," or "First Cry for Independence." Though it was not until May 1822 that Sucre's men defeated the Spanish, Ecuador's "Primer Grito de la Independencia" had inspired other Latin American colonies. Within the next few years, many others had won their independence

WORDS TO UNDERSTAND

Disillusioned: No longer believing in something or someone.

Effigy: A carved or sculpted representation of a person.

Superimpose: To place one image or thing over another, often so that both can still be seen.

◀ A dance group parades through the center of Santiago Chile in celebration of Independence Day.

from Spain. Most Latin American Independence Day celebrations feature parades of soldiers and students, speeches, official flag-raising ceremonies, and general frolicking.

All the islands of the Caribbean were colonies of European countries at some point in their histories, and a few, such as Aruba, the British Virgin Islands, and Martinique, are still closely tied to their colonizing countries. The United States has a presence in the Caribbean as well, in Puerto Rico and the United States Virgin Islands. In 1791, Haiti became the first Caribbean nation to gain independence from a European power, when the French leadership was overthrown by a slave rebellion. Fireworks, music, and dancing are part of many Caribbean independence celebrations.

■ Mes de la Patria in Chile

Chileans observe September 18 as Independence Day. On this day in 1810 they proclaimed independence from Spain (although they fought for eight more years to actually gain it). Even though Chile's Independence Day officially falls on September 18, Chileans celebrate their independence for the entire month of September, which they call *Mes de la Patria*, or "Month of the Nation." At the heart of the celebration are the five days surrounding September 18, during which people dance, eat, drink, and fly the Chilean flag.

Chileans love to hold barbecues called *asados*. At a family *asado*, the men build a fire and grill meats such as chicken, steak, and chorizo (spicy sausage) over it. Women assemble side dishes and get the tables ready while the children play. (*Asados* are often large affairs with lots of extended family and neighbors present, so there are usually many kids to play with.) The meal begins with *empanadas*, small meat pies, and bread with sausage in it. When the meat is ready, everyone eats. Diners linger over their meals for hours, drinking coffee and talking.

INDEPENDENCE DAY BARBECUES

Asados are popular in Argentina, which is famous for its beef cattle. The word *barbecue* comes from a Spanish word that originated during the 17th century: *barbacoa*.

People in Chile also like to go to *fondas* during their independence celebrations. A *fonda* is a gathering at which people eat, drink, and listen to live music and dance. Some *fondas* are held in dance halls or gymnasiums. Others are held in temporary open-air shelters roofed with eucalyptus branches, their dirt floors covered with sawdust. These *fondas* are usually open only from about September 16 to September 20. Every evening people gather to eat snacks, drink *chicha* (a kind of wine) or *pisco* (a kind of liquor made from grapes), and dance to live music.

Watch Chileans dance a traditional *cueca*.

The traditional Chilean musical style is called the *cueca*. A *cueca* is a poem sung in a complex pattern with many repetitions and added words. Musicians accompany the singer on guitars, harps, and drums. The *cueca* is also a dance performed by pairs of men and women who tie their steps to the sections of the song. The partners are not allowed to speak to or touch each other, and they are supposed to look into each other's eyes the entire time they are dancing (except when they are facing away from one another during turns). Each partner holds a handkerchief and waves it according to specific rules. Chilean kids have to learn to dance the *cueca* in school. Chileans who are really serious about dancing the *cueca* dress for the occasion, women in long black skirts and white blouses and men in riding pants, chaps, boots and spurs, short jackets, and ponchos. Both sexes wear flat-brimmed hats.

■ The First Cry in Ecuador

August 10 celebrates Ecuador's independence from Spain. After the "Primer Grito de la Independencia," there followed several years of fighting between Ecuadorian soldiers led by Antonio José de Sucre against the Spanish Royal army. In May 1822, Sucre's men defeated the Spanish at the Battle of Pichincha near Quito, in an event known as the Glorious May Revolution. This victory led to Spain granting Ecuador full independence. The country still celebrates its Independence Day on August 10, commemorating the first call for freedom. On this day Ecuadorians organize festivals, fairs, and bullfights. The national flag of three horizontal bands—yellow at the top (double width), blue in the middle, and red on the bottom, with the coat of arms **superimposed** at the center—is displayed all over the nation, and there is a military parade in the capital. Schools and public offices are closed and cultural events are held throughout the day. The evening is marked by public dinners.

■ Marching in El Salvador

El Salvador's Independence Day falls on September 15. El Salvador officially won its independence on September 15, 1821, after three centuries of Spanish rule. Every town and city celebrates by holding parades in the streets; in San Salvador, the capital, these parades take place at the city's largest stadium. Schools start preparing for the holiday well in advance. Every school chooses a group of students who will march into San Salvador on Independence Day. These students practice their parts for months. One student in each group carries the national flag. Behind that student come a marching band and dancers, followed by more marching students. On September 15, the students line up early in the morning, taking their places with the soldiers who also march in the parades. The parades start around 7 A.M. The students and soldiers march through the streets while the musicians play patriotic songs and the dancers dance. The national air force sends pilots to perform aerial acrobatics around the town as the parade progresses. After the parades are over, El Salvadorans like to go to the beach or a park to picnic, play, and relax for the rest of the day.

■ Schools Get into the Act in Guatemala

On September 15, 1821, Guatemala secured its independence from Spanish colonial rule. On the days leading up to the independence day holiday, banners of light blue and white (the colors of the national flag) are draped over all government buildings in the capital city. Students also decorate their schools in the national colors and schools hold assemblies at which children practice singing the national anthem. In the town of Antigua, school drum corps practice marching while playing their drums and xylophones so that they will be ready to march through the town's central park on Independence Day. Individual classes make up patriotic skits to perform on the holiday as well.

On the morning of September 15, the Guatemalan army performs ceremonial marching for the president and the air force shows off its aerobatic skills. The Guatemalan people throng the streets, many of them carrying small plastic flags. Towns hold celebrations that include folk dance competitions, performances of patriotic dramas, and displays of traditional arts and crafts.

■ Parades in Jamaica

Jamaica celebrates its independence from Britain on August 6. People parade along specified routes in colorful costumes. The parade normally has a large number of floats, a few disco units, dozens of **effigies** (figures or carvings), groups of costumed performers, and classic cars. Modern, as well as *junkanoo*, dancers showcase a cross-section of Jamaican culture. Prominent national leaders and cultural icons are featured in effigy, and models and sports personalities parade in the streets. Festival performers keep the atmosphere lively as they dance aboard the music trucks.

■ El Grito de Dolores in Mexico

Mexico declared independence from Spain on September 16, 1810. Celebrated as Mexico's Independence Day, September 16 is called El Grito de Dolores, or El Grito for short. It is also called El Grito de Independencia.

Spain ruled Mexico as a colony for almost 300 years. Hernán Cortés arrived in Mexico in 1521 and named the new colony Nueva España, or New Spain. The colony thrived, but as centuries passed, the people living in Mexico gradually became **disillusioned** with Spanish dominance. Influenced by the thinking of the Enlightenment that was sparking revolutions in other places the *criollos*, or Mexicans descended from Spanish parents, decided to seek their freedom.

On the morning of September 16, 1810, Father Miguel Hidalgo, leader of the *criollos*, rang a church bell in the town of Dolores signalling all Mexicans to fight for their freedom. He then made a speech to his followers in which he demanded independence from Spain; this was the *Grito de Dolores*, which began the 10-year war that finally resulted in Mexico becoming independent.

Mexico's Independence Day celebrations revolve around a reenactment of Hidalgo's bell-ringing. The festivities begin on the evening of September 15, when a government official rings the historic liberty bell and then shouts "Mexicanos, viva Mexico" ("Mexicans, long live Mexico"). This is an imitation of the cry of independence given by Father Hidalgo on that night in 1810. The president performs this ritual in Mexico City; in other cities, mayors or other officials perform the service. The crowd joins together to shout out the names of the men who fought for independence, followed by cries of "Viva México!" Finally, a massive display of fireworks lights up the sky.

The president waves the flag and the national anthem is sung. The next day is marked with civic ceremonies and the decoration of the statue of Father Hidalgo in Mexico City with flowers. There are rodeos, banquets, dances, bullfights, and horseback riding competitions in different regions of Mexico. Mexicans of all ages gather in town and city plazas dressed in traditional Mexican or indigenous costumes or in the national colors. Hundreds of vendors on the streets and in the plazas sell necessary supplies, such as sombreros, balloons, flags, and shuttlecocks (for playing badminton) in the national colors. Bands play mariachi music. Children line up to have their pictures taken sitting on a wooden horse, representing a cavalry steed. Everyone shouts and makes

AN AMERICAN HOLIDAY WITH MEXICAN ROOTS

The well-known holiday Cinco de Mayo, or May Fifth, is not Mexico's Independence Day, despite many people's mistaken belief that it is. Cinco de Mayo actually commemorates an 1862 battle in which a small army of Mexican farmers defeated the French army. The people of Puebla celebrate Cinco de Mayo, but other Mexicans ignore it. Cinco de Mayo is mainly a holiday celebrated in the United States to celebrate Mexican ancestry.

▲ Fireworks explode over the zocalo, or main square, during the celebration of Independence Day, in Culiacan City in Mexico's state of Sinaloa.

MARIACHI MUSIC

Mariachi is a type of music that is very popular in Mexico. A typical mariachi band includes a guitar, two trumpets, three violins, a bass called a *guitarrón*, and a high-pitched guitar called a *vihuela*. The musicians sing while they play. They often dress in traditional Mexican clothing, with broad-brimmed hats and silver-studded pants. Mariachi groups often perform at weddings, holiday festivals, and other special events.

noise with whistles, toy trumpets, and other noisemakers. Plazas become so packed with people that it is difficult to move.

Cars, streets, and houses are covered with the national colors of Mexico, green, white, and red. Nearly every building flies the Mexican flag. Cities and towns decorate their plazas with lighted decorations; the most spectacular decorations are in the zocalo, the main plaza of Mexico City. A military parade marches through Mexico City past the Hidalgo Memorial. People spend the day in the plazas, buying trinkets, listening to music, and eating. Hundreds of stands sell traditional snack foods, or *antojitos*. Popular snacks include enchiladas, tamales, quesadillas, and stuffed jalapeño peppers. Children especially love to drink *ponche*, a drink made of apples, raisins, *guayaba* (guava), and sugarcane.

Eating Beef in Paraguay

Independence Day in Paraguay commemorates the proclamation of its independence after the people of Paraguay overthrew the local Spanish authorities on May 15, 1811. On this day, the president presides over Independence Day celebrations in the capital of Asunción. The major highlights of these events include a presidential speech, a parade of the armed forces, and cultural exhibitions such as folk dances and folk music concerts. In Paraguay, holidays are an occasion to cook and eat festive foods. Popular dishes include breaded fried beef cutlets (called *milanesa*, in the style of the Italian city Milan); barbecued meat called *asado;* a beef soup with dumplings called *bori bori*; and a meat and rice pie called *so'o ku'i.*

Twenty-One-Cannon Salute in Peru

Peru's Independence Day, July 28, celebrates the country's liberation from Spain in 1824 by the Liberator, José de San Martin. Peruvians get two days off from school or work to celebrate the *Fiestas Patrias*, or Peruvian National Holidays. The celebrations begin on the evening of July 27, as

▲ Asado is a traditional method of roasting beef or other meats on a barbecue with vertical grills. In South American countries, such as Paraguay, it is a festive way to celebrate independence day and other holidays.

▲ A Peruvian police military band performs during an Independence Day parade in Lima, Peru.

musicians play concerts in city parks. July 28 is devoted to formal events. At dawn, the people of the capital city, Lima, are awakened by a 21-cannon salute. After a flag-raising ceremony, the president addresses the nation from the Congress hall. Next, each city holds a parade. All people, both military and civilian, march in these parades. Representatives from the army, navy, and air force, as well as from scout troops, schools, and other groups, all dress in uniform and march through the streets. Fireworks follow in the evening; the largest display is in the Plaza de Armas in Lima. On July 29, everyone rests after the festivities of the previous day. Families spend the day together eating, playing games, and going on outings to parks or the beach. Many families like to make trips to the interior of the country for picnics and hikes.

■ Multi-celebrations in St. Lucia

On February 22, 1979, St. Lucia became an independent country and a member of the British Commonwealth, a political and economic alliance of former British colonies. The islanders cherish their freedom. In St. Lucia, Independence Day is celebrated in conjunction with Carnival, Ash Wednesday, and Lent, traditional religious events related to Easter. A number of colorful events and parties are held each year to commemorate independence from Britain; these include parades, calypso music performances, and dance festivals. There are also special radio broadcasts, speeches made by politicians, and military parades on this day. Often royal dignitaries from the United Kingdom visit the island to mark Independence Day. Church services and school rallies are also held to express national pride.

Fireworks in Trinidad and Tobago

On Independence Day, celebrated on August 31, Trinidad and Tobago celebrate the anniversary of the end of their colonial status in 1962. Observances to mark Trinidad and Tobago's freedom from the United Kingdom include the president's address to the nation, a parade by the armed forces, and a huge display of fireworks at the capital, Port-of-Spain, in the evening. There are also performances by steel pan bands.

 TEXT-DEPENDENT QUESTIONS

1: What is a Chilean *asado*?

2: When did Mexico declare independence from Spain?

3: What is *ponche*, and where is it consumed?

 RESEARCH PROJECTS

1: Research the life of Father Miguel Hidalgo, including his early years, formation as a priest, and contributions to Mexican history. Write a biographical sketch that incorporates your findings as well as how he is remembered in Mexico today.

2: Research a poet from one of the Latin American countries profiled in this chapter. Investigate his or her work, themes, and reception in his or her country. Write a brief summary of the poet's life and work, being sure to include whether he or she has written verse on the theme of independence or revolution.

7

Celebrating in the Middle East

The region now known as the Middle East is home to the oldest literate civilizations in the world, with the earliest city-states appearing in Iraq some 5,000 years ago. Tremendous advances in science, technology, medicine, law, and astronomy were made by the people of this region, including the development of the first alphabet.

In the sixth century B.C.E. the Persians became the first rulers in the area to control a vast territory. In 333 B.C.E. the Greeks, under the leadership of Alexander the Great, defeated the Persians in the Battle of Issus. Over the next two years Persia's Mediterranean territories, Syria, Phoenicia (modern Lebanon), and Egypt fell to Alexander's army. By the end of 331 B.C.E., all of the Persian Empire was under his control. The Seleucids, the Greek rulers who followed Alexander, built their capital, Seleucia, to the south of modern Baghdad. They were overthrown by the Parthians in 138 B.C.E.

WORDS TO UNDERSTAND

Aliyah: The immigration of Jews to Israel from other countries.
Embroiled: Deeply involved in a tense or difficult situation.
Gregorian calendar: System of date keeping introduced by Pope Gregory XIII in 1582 and now the most widely used in the world today.

◀ A girl wearing traditional Omani dress attends national day celebrations at the Sultan Qaboos grand mosque in Oman.

From 226 C.E. until the middle of the seventh century the Sassanid dynasty ruled the region. The Sassanids and the neighboring Byzantine (Eastern Roman) Empire fought for control for more than 100 years. Sassanid rule lasted until 650 when the Arabs conquered Persia.

Under the Arab Umayyad caliphs, or leaders, Mesopotamia became a province of the Islamic empire. In 747, the Abbasids and other Umayyad enemies united and revolted against the Umayyads. After three years of fighting, the Abbasids took control of the region and Abu al-Abbas al-Saffah, the man who had organized the Abbasid revolution, became the first caliph of the Abbasid dynasty. During the Abbasid dynasty the Islamic empire achieved its golden age.

In 1453 the Ottoman Turks, who had gradually increased their territory since the 13th century, conquered Constantinople. Over the next 100 years they took control of Egypt, the coastline of the Red Sea, modern Israel, Jordan, Lebanon, Syria, Iraq, and a large area of southeastern Europe. Although the Safavids, who had come to power in Persia, fought the Ottomans for control over northern Iran and Iraq, as well as to extend control around the Caspian Sea and into Georgia, the Ottomans maintained power until the end of World War I, when France and England laid claim to Ottoman territory in many provinces.

Though the Middle East is home to the world's oldest civilizations, most of the nations in the region were formed during the 20th century. A number of the borders of the modern nations were drawn by Western powers with little regard to ethnic differences. As a result, ethnic groups that had fought one another for years have found themselves sharing national governments and territories. Other ethnic groups have been divided between a number of nations. To take just one example, the Kurdish people have their own language and customs, but their geographic homeland now exists in several different countries, including Turkey, Iran, Iraq, and Syria. This arbitrary division has resulted in years of fighting by Kurds who want their own homeland and other nations who have often tried to systematically suppress their culture.

The national divisions within the Middle East remain a source of conflict. In some cases, this can increase patriotism and enthusiasm for national day celebrations. In other cases, people feel that there is little cause for rejoicing. When people in the Middle East do observe national holidays, they celebrate by eating, drinking, listening to speeches, and watching parades.

■ Religious Revolution in Iran

On February 11 people in Iran celebrate their National Day, the anniversary of the Islamic Revolution in 1979. They also celebrate another national day, Islamic Republic Day on April 1. This day commemorates the beginning of the Islamic Republic of Iran also in 1979.

◀ Cheerful Iranian girls rally on Revolution Square to celebrate the establishment of the Islamic Republic on the eve of the National Day in Tehran, Iran's capital.

Before the revolution, Iran was ruled by a shah, a king, or emperor. In 1979 Ayatollah Khomeini, an Islamic religious leader, overthrew the shah and took over the country as supreme leader. On April 1, 1979, the people of Iran went to the polls for the first time and voted in favor of an Islamic republican system. The nation was transformed from a monarchy into an Islamic republic, with its laws derived from Islamic teachings. Since then the government has become much more conservative and imposed a number of rules on the people. For example, boys and girls can no longer attend school together, and women have to cover themselves with veils when they go out in public.

Despite the strict rules governing their behavior, the Iranian people still enjoy celebrating their Independence Day. Cities hold parades and families go on picnics in parks, where they eat festive foods such as lamb or chicken stew, nuts and dried fruits, and egg omelets called *kuku*. At night Iranians enjoy watching fireworks displays.

■ Yom Ha'atzmaut in Israel

Israel is the only Jewish state in the world. The Jewish people originated in Israel and the surrounding area during biblical times, but for thousands of years they have been dispersed throughout the world. Even living in the Diaspora, however, Jews never gave up their belief that the Land of Israel, a region that includes most of modern Israel and the city of Jerusalem, was their homeland,

MCFALAFEL

A favorite holiday snack in Israel is falafel, made of ground chickpeas mixed with onion and spices, shaped into balls, and then fried. In Egypt, McDonald's serves a falafel sandwich–called a McFalafel of course.

given to them by God. Jews began moving back into Israel in the 1880s, in a process known as *aliyah*. After World War I, the British government began working toward the creation of a Jewish state. Israel declared its independence on May 14, 1948, and ever since then has celebrated its nationhood around that date. The state of Israel has endured almost constant conflict with its Arab neighbors, who dispute the Jewish claim to this land.

Israel's Independence Day, called Yom Ha'atzmaut, is celebrated on the Tuesday, Wednesday, or Thursday that falls the closest to the fifth day of the month of Iyar in the Jewish calendar. This means that the holiday falls sometime between April 15 and May 15 on the **Gregorian calendar**, the calendar used by the Western world. Independence day celebrations begin at sundown on the fourth day of Iyar. (In the Jewish calendar a day begins at sundown, as opposed to starting at midnight.)

At sundown, the day's beginning, the speaker of the Knesset (the Israeli parliament) gives a speech at Mount Herzl, a hilltop and national cemetery in Jerusalem. Soldiers display their marching skills, arranging themselves in formations that look like Jewish symbols such as menorahs, seven-branched candelabras that are used to celebrate the Jewish holiday Hanukkah. Honored citizens light 12 torches, one for each of the traditional 12 tribes of Israel. The government awards an Israel

▲ The weather is fine and spirits are high as parks, forests, and nature reserves fill with Israelis celebrating the nation's independence with a traditional barbecue at HaYarkon Park in Tel Aviv.

Prize for that year to those who have made substantial contributions to the humanities, Jewish studies, science, and other categories. Yom Ha'atzmaut celebrations are especially intense because Israel is perpetually in conflict with its Arab neighbors, who dispute the nation's right to exist.

Almost everyone living in Israel celebrates on Yom Ha'atzmaut. Parties and concerts attract many revelers, but the most popular activity is barbecuing. Families set up small portable grills in parks and on beaches. These grills burn charcoal, which is kept alight by energetic fanning with pieces of cardboard, Ping-Pong paddles, electric hair dryers, or any other item than can create a breeze. Parks are so full of families having picnics that scarcely a blade of grass can be seen. The roads throughout Israel are clogged with cars traveling to Independence Day festivities.

■ Not Feeling Very Independent in Lebanon

Lebanon's Independence Day is November 22. On this day in 1943 Lebanon won its freedom from the League of Nations mandate under French administration. It is a public holiday from school and work. Most years, Lebanese people celebrate with a military parade, flag-raising ceremonies, public speeches, and other festivities that crowd the streets.

In November 2007, however, the streets were empty and celebrations meager. Lebanon was **embroiled** in a political crisis caused by strife between its neighbors, Israel and Syria. The president, Emile Lahoud, was about to leave office, and it was not clear who would succeed him. Syria and Iran were pressing for one candidate favorable to them. The United States and Saudi Arabia preferred a different candidate favorable to Israel. A Beirut newspaper (Beirut is the capital and chief port of Lebanon) ran an Independence Day cartoon depicting a Lebanese flag half covered by the flags of Syria, Iran, Egypt, Russia, France, and the United States, with an empty Lebanese presidential throne. The overwhelming feeling in the country was that Lebanon was not really independent and had little to celebrate.

After several years of discord within the government, Michel Aoun was elected president of Lebanon in 2016. When he assumed office, the country had not had a president in over two years. Aoun attended Lebanon's Independence Day festivities in Beirut soon after he took office.

■ Three Days of Holiday in Qatar

National Day, or Independence Day, celebrates Qatar's independence from the United Kingdom in 1971. To celebrate this anniversary, people in Qatar stop working for three days, from September 3 to 5. On August 25, the government starts decorating buildings with lights and designs. Qataris tend not to travel on this holiday, instead choosing to spend it close to home with their families.

▲ The Lebanese Prime Minister presides over a military parade in Beirut to mark the anniversary of Lebanon's independence.

On September 1, Qataris begin celebrating by dancing a traditional dance called *al arda*. The morning of September 3, most people in Qatar flock to the royal palace to see the country's leader, the amir. At noon, the air force puts on a show of aerobatics, and that evening, people crowd into restaurants to eat traditional foods; one popular dish is *mashboss*, a mixture of rice, vegetables, and meat. The next two days find Qatiris eating, drinking, and celebrating at home and on the streets.

Check out scenes of National Day in Qatar.

■ Sword Dance in Saudi Arabia

Saudi Arabia's Independence Day is September 23, which marks the date in 1932 on which the kingdom was unified. For this reason it is also called Unification Day. The Saudi Islamic Cultural Center (ICC) officially celebrates the occasion by organizing their national dance, the *ardha*, or "sword dance" functions. The *ardha* is performed by men. It originated in the plateau region of Najd, located in northern Saudi Arabia. The dance involves men dancing to the sounds of a poet narrator and a drummer. In the *ardha* dance, the poet begins singing, the drummer beats the drum, and the men begin dancing with their shoulders touching.

Festivals and Candy in Syria

In Syria, schools close on April 17 to celebrate its independence from the League of Nations mandate under French administration in 1946. To celebrate the liberation from French occupation, the Syrian government holds mass rallies, and the nation's leaders address the general public. Children and adults attend street festivals, where they eat, drink, and play games. The Military Museum and the Martyr's Monument are also open for visitors on this day. Many exhibits in the fields of art, technology, and culture are held on Syrian National Day as well. In the evening, cities hold fireworks and air shows, and candy and ice cream companies give away free samples to advertise their products. Sadly, a civil war broke out in Syria in 2011. It has had devastating effects on the country's population, infrastructure, and ability to celebrate cultural events such as National Day.

First Arabic Opera Produced in United Arab Emirates

On December 2, 1971, the United Arab Emirates (UAE) was formed, independent from the United Kingdom. To mark the anniversary of this event, there are many celebrations all across the federation. Parades are held on this day to celebrate the achievements of the country since it was founded. In the United Arab Emirates, National Day is a national holiday and schools and businesses are closed. Many sporting events, such as cricket, are also organized on this day. There are also shows, concerts, and fireworks.

In 2007, many Emiratis attended a program called Live Dubai 2007, which featured performances of music, poetry, and storytelling, an exhibition of the biggest businesses in the UAE, and a big dinner. The highlight of the event was a performance of the world's first Arabic opera, *Glorious Wedding*, which tells the history of the UAE and its development into a modern economic powerhouse, particularly in trade and real estate on both domestic and international fronts.

Building on the success of the inaugural event, Live Dubai 2008 featured dance, music, and poetry presentations to celebrate the nation's tremendous progress and growth from modest origins only 37 years before. Subsequent celebrations have included parades, celebrity-studded concerts, and fireworks displays.

In a typical celebration of national feeling, the students of Dubai's Zayed University recently held their own national day festivities. Activities included hot air balloon rides, traditional dances, animal shows, and displays of old coins and stamps. Some students dressed in traditional costumes. A market sold cultural items and the proceeds went to charity. In addition, a band played *liwa*, a local musical style in which men stand in a circle surrounding a man playing a reed instrument. Three men play drums while the other participants dance in their circle. The most

▲ Since schools and many businesses are closed on National Day, families gather to enjoy holiday meals.

popular event at Zayed University's celebration was a recitation of the national anthem–in Arabic–by Japanese students at the university–from a hot air balloon! Students at nearby Dubai Women's College held their own festival with parades, poetry readings, *yola* (a type of rifle shooting), and skydiving. The students at both universities enjoyed the opportunity to think about their nation and build national pride. The colleges encouraged even foreign students and staff members to dress in Arab clothing.

■ National Pride in Yemen

On May 22, 1990, Yemen was reunified and proclaimed a republic. The Republic of Yemen was established by merging North Yemen (Yemen Arab Republic) and South Yemen (People's Democratic Republic of Yemen). North Yemen had become independent in November 1918 from the Ottoman Empire, while South Yemen became independent much later, on November 30, 1967, from the United Kingdom. On this day Yemen also decided to adopt democracy. The new Yemeni constitution that was implemented on May 22 stressed the protection of human rights and freedoms, such as freedom of the press and expression. May 22 is celebrated as National Unity Day. On this day the Yemeni national flag, three horizontal bands of red, white, and black, is unfurled and a patriotic fervor grips the entire nation.

TEXT-DEPENDENT QUESTIONS

1: In what battle did the Greeks defeat the Persians in 333 B.C.E.?

2: What is the official name of Israel's Independence Day?

3: When was the United Arab Emirates formed?

RESEARCH PROJECTS

1: Research key events in the history of the Ottoman Empire, from its inception in 1299 through its dissolution in 1922. Create a timeline of these events accompanied by brief descriptions. Be sure to include noteworthy figures and contributions to world culture.

2: Research one of the ancient civilizations of the Middle East. Examples include the Sumerians, Babylonians, and Assyrians. Write a brief overview of the civilization, including key contributions to the fields of law, writing and language, science, and others.

8

Celebrating in North America

Every July the United States celebrates its courage in declaring itself independent and fighting for its freedom against the British, while Canada rejoices in its own independence (granted by the Canada Act) and its national **prosperity**.

■ Canada

Canadians celebrate their national day on Canada Day, July 1. The eastern half of Canada was a British colony for hundreds of years. On July 1, 1867, the British North American Act joined the provinces of Nova Scotia, New Brunswick, and Canada into a federation with its own constitution. Canada was not an independent nation at that

WORDS TO UNDERSTAND

Dominion: An entity of the British Empire or commonwealth that functioned independently but still acknowledged the British monarch as head of state.

Prosperity: A state of financial or material success.

Siege: When military forces surround a specific place to cut off the flow of supplies.

◀ Canada Day Fireworks illuminate the Peace Tower on Parliament Hill in Ottawa, the country's capital.

point. The British North America Act made it a **dominion**, which meant that Canada governed itself independently but was still part of the British Commonwealth.

The Canadian government proclaimed July 1 a national holiday in 1879, calling it Dominion Day. In its early years, Dominion Day was not a major holiday. In the 1950s the Canadian government started organizing Dominion Day celebrations that included band concerts, fireworks, and a military ceremony known as Trooping the Colours on Parliament Hill in Ottawa. In this ceremony, regiments of the army assemble on a field with their individual flags. The regiments take turns marching past the entire assembly so that all the soldiers learn each other's colors, which makes it easier for them to recognize one another in battle.

Dominion Day became more popular after Canada's centennial in 1967. In 1982, the Canada Act made Canada an independent nation, free of ties to the United Kingdom. Dominion Day's name was changed to Canada Day. Since 1985, each Canadian province has coordinated its own Canada Day celebrations, with assistance from the national government.

Canadians celebrate their national day with a range of local festivals. Many cities and towns sponsor parades and carnivals to mark the day. Canadians everywhere sing their national anthem, "O Canada!" Air shows and boating demonstrations are also popular spectacles. Canadian flags hang everywhere and people walk around wearing red and white shirts or shirts depicting red maple leaves. (The Canadian flag is red and white, with a red maple leaf located in the center.)

In Ottawa, huge crowds gather at Parliament Hill to watch the Changing of the Guard, listen to speeches by the prime minister, watch the Canadian flag being raised, and eat, drink, and play games. Many Canadians like to attend pancake breakfasts on the morning of Canada Day. Free concerts are held throughout the day and huge fireworks displays at night. Recent celebrations featured the SkyHawks, Canada's parachute demonstration team, dropping skydivers into Jacques-Cartier Park. Cirque Fantastic Concept, a team of circus artists, also performed a spectacular blend of acrobatics, dance, music, and theater. Celebrations are held at other parks around the city as well.

CREATING FOR CANADA

In 2017, the Canadian government celebrated the 30th anniversary of the Canada Day Challenge. Canadians ages 8 to 18 are invited to submit drawings, photos, or pieces of writing. The creators of the most dynamic work receive prizes such as a trip to Ottawa, the national capital, and tours of parliamentary buildings and museums. The contest has drawn some 350,000 entrants since it began in 1987.

▲ A man dressed up for Canada Day sells flags to a family.

FUN FOR KIDS AT JACQUES-CARTIER PARK, OTTAWA, ONTARIO

Past events of Canada Day celebrations at Ottawa's popular Jacques-Cartier Park have included a running race for kids, face painting, inflatable games, chalk drawing on pavement, demonstrations of aboriginal carving, a craft fest where kids could make their own Canada Day souvenirs, a fishing camp, hands-on science activities, a dance stage, and a drum circle. There have even been "voyageur" games to teach children about Canada's fur trade.

SMALL-TOWN FUN IN SOOKE, BRITISH COLUMBIA

The Canada Day celebration in Sooke, British Columbia, is a good place to go to enjoy western Canadian traditions. The Sooke Loggers' Sports Club demonstrates the craft of chopping wood, cutting with chainsaws, and throwing axes. Dogs show off their obedience and skill at the Canine Agility Demonstration. Activities include a craft fair, bingo, a parade by the Sooke Pipe and Drums corps, sack races and three-legged races, an inflatable play zone, face painting, and karaoke. Food vendors sell hamburgers, donuts, souvlaki (shish kebab), gelato (a soft rich ice cream), and pizza. Anyone who is not full from those snacks and the free Canada Day Cake offered on this day may want to participate in the pie-eating contest, always a popular spectator sport.

EATING CONTESTS

For some reason, Independence Day and Canada Day have become occasions for eating contests. Pie-eating contests are common in fairs throughout both the United States and Canada. Contestants keep their hands behind their backs and shove their faces into pies, chewing and swallowing as fast as they can, as their faces become covered with fruit and crust.

■ United States

The United States celebrates its Independence Day on July 4, known as the Fourth of July. Independence Day commemorates the date on which the Second Continental Congress (a group of Americans intent on forming a new nation) adopted the Declaration of Independence, in which "the thirteen united States of America" declared their independence from their colonial ruler, Great Britain. The Congress actually resolved to declare independence on July 2, but the Declaration was officially adopted on July 4.

▲ Three teenage girls dressed in red, white, and blue sing patriotic tunes atop a parade float.

The East Coast of North America had been claimed by England as British colonies during the 17th and 18th centuries. By the 1770s, many of these colonists had come to believe that they should be an independent nation, owing no obligation and paying no taxes to England. The Declaration of Independence, written almost entirely by Thomas Jefferson, outlined the colonists' complaints about British domination and listed the rights that they believed they deserved. On July 4, 1776, the Declaration was adopted, announcing that they were forming an independent nation.

Ever since that day, the United States has considered July 4 to be the date of its founding. The very next year, 1777, Americans began celebrating the day with parades, fireworks, 13-gun salutes, readings of the Declaration, and speeches. The states gradually made July 4 an official

▲ Backyard family barbecues are a favorite way to celebrate the Fourth of July holiday.

holiday, but it was not until 1870 that it became a federal holiday (although even then, workers still did not get paid if they took the day off). It was not until 1941 that the Fourth of July became a paid federal holiday.

Today Independence Day is a major holiday throughout the United States. Most federal and state institutions close, and there is no mail delivery. Cities and towns, schools, shopping centers, and other businesses decorate with American flags and banners in red, white, and blue, the flag's colors. Many towns hold parades during the day. Americans have barbecues and picnics and enjoy the weather outdoors. Fireworks displays are everywhere.

▲ Fireworks illuminate the Charles River during the Boston Harborfest celebrations.

INDEPENDENCE DAY IN BOSTON, MASSACHUSETTS

As the site of the Boston Tea Party (a protest by colonists against the British government in 1773) and several early battles in the American Revolution, Boston puts on one of the most spectacular Independence Day spectacles in the United States. Called Harborfest, celebrations last several days and attract more than 2.5 million visitors. Tourists and locals enjoy taking historical tours, watching reenactments of Revolutionary events, and eating clam chowder at the Chowderfest, a competition among restaurants for the title "Boston's Best Chowder." The highlight of Harborfest is the Boston Pops Orchestra Fireworks Spectacular, at which the fireworks company, Pyro Spectaculars, use more than 20,000 pounds of explosives, including shells 10 inches in diameter, to illuminate the Charles River, which separates Boston from its Charlestown port and the city of Cambridge. The company imports specialty fireworks from around the world, including such pyrotechnic powerhouses as China and Japan. Spectators crowd the Esplanade, a long level area that runs along the Charles River, lining up to enter the area the day before the holiday. On the evening of July 4, the Boston Pops Orchestra plays a concert of patriotic songs while the fireworks light up the sky.

JULY 4 IN NEW YORK CITY, NEW YORK

New York City's Fourth of July celebrations attract millions of locals and tourists. Visitors can watch Independence Day parades; visit Revolutionary War sites such as Fort Greene Park in Brooklyn, the Brooklyn Bridge, and the Morris-Jumel Mansion in Harlem; or relax and play Frisbee in Central Park in Manhattan. Eating events are also popular. One of the most famous eating events is the Nathan's Famous Fourth of July International Hot Dog Eating

Enjoy scenes of New York City's famous Fourth of July fireworks display.

Contest, which takes place every July 4 in Coney Island in Brooklyn.

Contestants line up to devour hot dogs. They have 12 minutes to consume as many hot dogs as they can (the hot dog buns also need to be eaten). For several years in the 2000s the champion hot dog-eater was a Japanese man named Takeru Kobayashi, whose technique of folding the dogs in half and dipping the buns in water seemed to make him unstoppable. However, in 2007, nursing a jaw injury, Kobayashi lost to Californian Joey Chestnut. Chestnut was able to eat 66 hot dogs, while Kobayashi only managed 63. Chestnut went on to win eight straight titles through the year 2014. He lost in 2015 but recaptured the title in 2016. In 2017 he won again by eating 72 hot dogs.

▲ Competition is fierce in the Nathan's Famous annual Fourth of July International Hot Dog Eating Contest in New York City.

In the evening, multiple fireworks displays light up the sky over the five boroughs of New York. The department store Macy's sponsors fireworks throughout the city, including over the East River and at South Street Seaport. As some of the best views are from boats, several boat companies offer fireworks cruises for those who manage to book early.

TEXT- DEPENDENT QUESTIONS

1: What was the result of the British North America Act in Canada?

2: Who wrote the majority of the American Declaration of Independence?

3: What year did the Fourth of July became a paid federal holiday?

RESEARCH PROJECTS

1: Select a Canadian city not profiled in this chapter, such as Toronto, Montreal, or Vancouver. Find out activities happening for this year's Canada Day. Create a brochure outlining each of these events and including brief descriptions.

2: Research Native American responses and reactions to Independence Day. Write a brief summary of different perspectives, including any alternate ways Native American groups might choose to mark the day.

9

Celebrating in Oceania

The term *Oceania* refers to a vast expanse of islands in the tropical and the subtropical regions of the Pacific Ocean. The islands of Oceania are divided into three main groups–Melanesia, Micronesia, and Polynesia. They are differentiated by the physical characteristics of the islands, as well as the inhabitants on them. The countries of Oceania include Australia, New Zealand, the Marshall Islands, Federated States of Micronesia, Papua New Guinea, Samoa, and Tonga.

The nations of Oceania have a wide variety of national celebrations. Some of them never actually became independent, or achieved independence very gradually, such as Australia. These nations often celebrate national days or constitution days instead. Others commemorate events such as their liberation from wartime domination.

WORDS TO UNDERSTAND

Autonomous: Independent and self-governing.

Bicentennial: An anniversary of two hundred years.

Boycott: To decline to attend an event or purchase a product as a form of protest.

◄ Children compete in the annual Australia Day watermelon-eating contest at the Coogee Beach Festival in Coogee, Western Australia.

■ Public Celebrations in Australia

Australians celebrate their nation on Australia Day, January 26. Since Australia gradually became independent from the United Kingdom over the course of the 20th century, the country has no clear independence day. Australia Day instead commemorates the colonization of Australia. The first English ships full of colonists, the First Fleet, landed in Sydney Harbor in January 1788. The First Fleet discharged its passengers (mostly male convicts) and raised the English flag on January 26.

The first years of the Australia colony were extremely difficult, and many of the original settlers died. Many more survived, however, and England kept shipping new loads of convicts to Australia both to increase its European population there, and to rid England of the convicts. On January 26, 1808, the colony's leaders held a celebration to recognize that the British colony had survived 20 years. They called the day "Foundation Day," or "First Landing." Starting in 1818, the government declared January 26 a holiday for government workers. Other businesses followed suit.

By the end of the 19th century most of Australia celebrated January 26 as "Anniversary Day." During the 20th century, the name gradually changed to "Australia Day." In 1946, all the individual governments of Australia agreed to celebrate Australia Day on January 26. If January 26 falls on a

▲ The tall ship *James Cook* makes its way past the Sydney Opera House during the Australia Day harbor review.

weekend, the following Monday is observed as a public holiday. Today, Australia day is celebrated throughout Australia. The National Australia Day Council, based in Sydney, is the government organization charged with organizing public festivities.

FIREWORKS OVER SYDNEY

In Sydney, events begin at dawn and stretch until after dark at Hyde Park. The day begins with a ceremony featuring political speeches and the playing of the national anthem, the Oz Day 10K run, and discounted entries to local museums. A fleet of vintage double-decker buses from the Sydney Bus Museum offers visitors rides through the city. Visitors to Darling Harbor enjoy free entertainment for children, an international food fair, and a parade of boats in the water. The Australia Day Spectacular is a multimedia event of music, lights, pyrotechnics, and a fireworks display over Cockle Bay.

AUSTRALIA'S BICENTENNIAL

Australia Day in 1988 was a major celebration, commemorating the bicentennial of the First Fleet's arrival in Australia. The celebrations were centered on the country's largest city, Sydney, but every part of Australia held its own festivities.

PUPPET SHOWS AND FACE PAINTING IN BRISBANE, QUEENSLAND

In Brisbane, the state capital of Queensland, the main celebrations are held at South Bank Parklands. There are free circus workshops and face painting for children, puppet shows, and performances by African rhythm ensembles and swing bands. In 2014, the Australia Day Multi-Faith Ceremony was held at Elder Hall, one of Australia's most notable concert venues located in the city of Adelaide. Representatives from eight different faiths were in attendance.

BUCKING BRONCOS IN TASMANIA

In Tasmania, local governments organize community breakfasts and award ceremonies, outdoor movies, and dance parties on Australia day. The Ulverstone Rodeo, held on January 26, is the biggest rodeo in Tasmania and one of the top 10 biggest in Australia. Cowboys travel from all over Tasmania and from mainland Australia to participate. They ride bucking broncos, try to tame wild bulls, and show off precision riding. Clowns and comedians also perform. In the evening after the rodeo, the competitors join the parade that rolls down the main street of Ulverstone.

AUSTRALIA'S ABORIGINES PROTEST NATIONAL DAY

Australia's Aborigines, native inhabitants of the continent, call Australia Day "Invasion Day." From their perspective, January 26 was the day on which invading Europeans began taking over their land and destroying their native culture. They have protested this day for many years. In 1938, Aborigines held their own day of mourning on Australia Day. In 1988, Aborigines held a concert at the Bondi Pavilion in Sydney protesting the treatment of Aborigines at the hands of Europeans. They also opened an embassy at which European Australians could meet Aborigines and hear from them about the needs of the Aboriginal people. Many Aborigines still find the idea of Australia Day repulsive and continue to **boycott** celebrations or hold their own events to draw attention to the way they have been mistreated. A number of Australians of European descent, too, are uncomfortable celebrating Australia Day because of the effect that European colonization had on the indigenous Australians.

▲ The Sydney Opera House is one of Australia's most recognizable landmarks. Here, as part of Australia Day celebrations, the sails of the opera house are illuminated to celebrate the country's Aboriginal culture.

The Australian government has been attempting to make peace with the indigenous population. On Australia Day, it now holds a special ceremony called the Woggan ma gule Morning Ceremony. In this ceremony native Australians perform songs, dances, and traditional rituals designed to honor the spirits of Aboriginal ancestors. It is performed in the Royal Botanic Gardens, which were formerly the sacred land of the Gadigal Aboriginal people. Many Aborigines participate in and watch this ceremony. A number of white Australians also attend, finding this the best way to celebrate their nation and the rich heritage of the indigenous people.

■ Waitangi Day in New Zealand

Like Australia, New Zealand gradually gained independence from the British during the 19th and 20th centuries, so the country has no single independence day. New Zealand does, however, have a national day. On February 6, 1840, the Treaty of Waitangi, New Zealand's founding document, was signed. This day, Waitangi Day, is commemorated each year.

OCEANIC NATIONAL DAY CELEBRATION IN LONDON, ENGLAND

London, England, is the site of an Oceanic national day celebration. The New Zealanders in London on February 6, Waitangi Day, celebrate the occasion by going on a pub crawl. They spend the day and evening riding the London Underground's Circle Line from pub to pub, drinking beer and celebrating with fellow Kiwis (New Zealanders). They also sing patriotic songs and wear distinctive outfits such as rugby shirts or sheep costumes. At 4 P.M. they gather at Westminster for a *haka*, a traditional Maori dance. Observers comment that this celebration is much livelier (perhaps thanks to all the beer drunk in pubs) than the festivities that usually occur in New Zealand on the same day.

The Treaty of Waitangi was made between the chiefs of the Maori, New Zealand's indigenous people, and the British government. It made New Zealand a part of the British Empire and granted the Maori certain rights of citizenship.

The people of New Zealand first celebrated Waitangi Day as a national holiday in 1934. It was organized by European and Maori descendants of the original signers of the Treaty of Waitangi. Thousands of New Zealanders of both races attended the celebrations. Speakers prayed that the two races might unite as one nation, though in this case they specified that this should happen through Christianity.

Waitangi Day gradually became an annual event. In 1953 the queen of England attended. February 6 became an official public holiday in 1974. On the morning of Waitangi Day, the navy raises New Zealand's flag at the Waitangi Treaty Grounds overlooking the Bay of Islands. At a church service, entertainers sing songs and perform native dances. Some people attend concerts. Political leaders give speeches both at the Treaty Grounds and at other celebrations around New Zealand. Many New Zealanders spend Waitangi Day at the beach.

▲ Waka boats take part in the Waitangi Day paddling regatta in New Zealand. The day commemorates the 1840 signing of the Treaty of Waitangi, which guaranteed Maori tribal rights in exchange for British sovereignty over New Zealand.

Ever since the first Waitangi Day, controversy has surrounded the holiday. The Maori people do not agree with the way Waitangi Day celebrations portray the history of the nation. In particular, they believe the Treaty of Waitangi promised them land rights that they have not been granted. In the 1940s Maori leaders boycotted the celebrations. In the 1970s they began to demand that the government end racial discrimination and grant them their land rights. During the 1980s, Maori protesters disrupted the speeches at Waitangi Day celebrations. Celebrations during the 1990s proved complicated, with organizers trying to accommodate various groups who all had different opinions about the nature of the day. Today, Maori activists still use Waitangi Day as an opportunity to protest government policies.

■ Papua New Guinea

Papua New Guinea became an independent nation on September 16, 1975, parting from Australia's government. More than 30 heads of state from other countries arrived to celebrate the country's independence, the majority reaching the country a few days in advance, on September 14, so as to join in the merrymaking. On the day itself, they assembled at Sogeri National High School for the flag-raising ceremony.

The students and teachers dressed in special outfits in colors representing the 20 provinces of the nation. The whole group went to Independence Hill to unveil and raise the new Papua New Guinea flag. Later that day, ceremonies were held at the Sir Hubert Murray Stadium, located in Port Moresby, the capital city of Papua New Guinea. The new government signed its constitution, swore in its new members of Parliament, and gave local gifts to the visiting dignitaries. Dancers performed traditional dances, and the Sogeri

BOUGAINVILLE

The Bougainville province has long struggled for independence from Papua New Guinea. It declared itself independent on September 1, 1975, calling itself the Republic of the North Solomons. The governments of Australia and Papua New Guinea refused to recognize this declaration, and the Bougainville region has remained part of New Guinea since that time. The Bougainville Revolutionary Army fought with Papuan forces for a number of years, seeking independence. Finally in 1997 New Zealand negotiated a peace agreement, and in 2000 Bougainville was established as an autonomous region with its own government. During the many years of conflict, the people of Bougainville continued to hold Independence Day celebrations on September 1 and to hope that they would one day be truly independent.

high school students put on a play depicting the history of Papua New Guinea from the pre-colonial period to the present day.

The prime minister usually addresses the people of Papua New Guinea on Independence Day and says encouraging words about the progress the nation has made, and can still make in the future. Today, Independence Day is a time for the people of Papua New Guinea to celebrate their old traditions as well as the modernization of their country. Many people dress in traditional costumes made of feathers, plant materials, shells, and bone. They may paint their faces in colorful patterns as well.

■ Pacific Islands

The island nations of the South Pacific spent most of the 19th and 20th centuries under the domination of stronger nations, particularly the United Kingdom, the United States, and Japan. Many of them gained independence during the late 20th century. For them, Independence Day celebrations are a time to reflect on the progress their new nations have made and the progress they still hope to make.

One feature of many Pacific island national day festivals is outrigger canoe racing in the ocean. Outriggers are long, thin, canoe-shaped objects that are attached several feet to the side of a canoe, running parallel with the hull. The outrigger helps stabilize the boat in rough seas and makes it less likely to capsize. Though islanders have made outrigger canoes for centuries, today's outrigger canoes are extremely high-tech crafts made with modern materials such as aluminum. In outrigger canoe races, between one and 12 people take paddles and sit in a line facing the front of the canoe. The steerer sits in the back of the canoe and steers with a paddle or a rudder. The paddlers lean over the side (but not far enough for the boat to capsize) and paddle together to propel the boat to the finish line. Races can be very short, such as sprints of 250 meters, or long open-water treks between islands.

INDEPENDENCE CELEBRATED ALL WEEK IN FIJI

Fiji became independent from the United Kingdom on October 10, 1970. Today October 10 is known as Fiji Day. Fiji Day comes at the end of a week of celebrations known as Fiji Week. Events include concerts, games and activities for children, organized walks through the park, and numerous political speeches.

INDEPENDENCE IN KIRIBATI

Kiribati became independent from British control on July 12, 1979. Since then it has celebrated July 12 as its Independence Day. Kiribati celebrates the event with a colorful parade, and a review of troops, followed by various field events such as soccer, basketball, tennis, and volleyball matches, as well as marathons and canoe races. There are also fishing tournaments, dance competitions, and a band competition. All educational and government establishments remain closed.

CONSTITUTION DAY DRAWS VISITORS TO MARSHALL ISLANDS

The government of the Marshall Islands enacted its constitution on May 1, 1979. Since then, the Marshallese people have celebrated Constitution Day on May 1. Thousands of people gather annually at the Capital Complex to watch parades and listen to bands. Participants come from all over the nation, including groups from schools, churches, and individual islands. Representatives from other countries visit as well; for the 25th anniversary celebration, for example, visitors traveled from Kiribati, the Federated States of Micronesia, China, Japan, Australia, Indonesia, Papua New Guinea, Tuvalu, Thailand, New Zealand, Germany, Austria, Vatican City, and the United States.

DANCING AND FEASTING IN FEDERATED STATES OF MICRONESIA

On May 10, 1979, the districts of Micronesia ratified a new constitution and created a new nation, the Federated States of Micronesia, with the United States functioning as trustee. May 10 is now Micronesia's Constitution Day. Micronesia also has an Independence Day, November 3. On November 3, 1986, the United States ended its trusteeship of the Federated States of Micronesia. From that point on, the nation was completely self-governing.

Both of these dates are national holidays. Politicians give speeches, and the people hold sports tournaments and canoe races. The islanders also dance, sing, and feast on traditional foods.

BEAUTY PAGEANT IN THE NORTHERN MARIANA ISLANDS

The Northern Mariana Islands are not an independent nation. Instead, they function as a commonwealth in political union with the United States. (In this context, a commonwealth is an unincorporated territory; the islands govern themselves but the U.S. government provides some guidance and funding.) The constitution of the commonwealth took effect on January 1, 1978, and since then Commonwealth Day has been celebrated every January.

The people of the Marianas also celebrate July 4, Independence Day in the United States, as Liberation Day. Commemorating the liberation of the islands by

Learn about dance traditions in Tonga.

the Americans from the Japanese during World War II, Liberation Day is a much bigger festival than Commonwealth Day. Festivities go on for several days and end on July 4. In Saipan, a carnival at the American Memorial Park lasts for most of June with games and activities for children, as well as bands, entertainers, and food booths. Many people think that the highlight of Liberation Day is the Miss Liberation Day beauty pageant, at which the Miss Liberation Day Queen is crowned. A parade closes the festivities on July 4.

DANCING AND FEASTING IN TONGA

Tonga became fully independent from the United Kingdom on June 4, 1970. Tongans now celebrate June 4 as Emancipation Day, dressing in traditional clothing, and dancing, singing, and feasting. Many Tongans eat sitting on mats on the floor, even at feasts. Children usually do not eat with adults. The people of Tonga enjoy traditional dancing and singing at festivals. The *lakalaka* is a line dance performed by men and women who tell stories of historical events. Young women perform dances to love songs called *hiva kakala*. The *kailao* is a war dance. Tongan poets compose new songs with complicated harmonies for these dances. Emancipation Day is also observed with processions, parades, and public speeches.

TEXT-DEPENDENT QUESTIONS

1: Name the three main groups of islands of Oceania.

2: Why do Australia's Aborigines call Australia Day "Invasion Day"?

3: What is the name of New Zealand's founding document?

RESEARCH PROJECTS

1: Research the Torres Strait Islanders, another indigenous group of Australia separate from the Aborigines. Write a brief overview of their history and culture, including facts about their language, location, art, and other information.

2: Research the various countries that have claimed, occupied, or otherwise governed the Marshall Islands, as well as the historical circumstances of each change in power. Create a timeline of this history with relevant details.

▲ A group of young men performs a traditional dance for Emancipation Day in Tonga.

Series Glossary

ancestors The direct family members of one who is deceased

aristocrat A member of a high social class, the nobility, or the ruling class

atonement The act of making up for sins so that they may be forgiven

ayatollah A major religious leader, scholar, and teacher in Shii Islam; the religious leader of Iran

colonial era A period of time between the 17th to 19th century when many countries of the Americas and Africa were colonized by Europeans.

colonize To travel to and settle in a foreign land that has already been settled by groups of people. To colonize can mean to take control of the indigenous groups already in the area or to wield power over them in order to control their human and physical resources.

commemorate To honor the memory of a person or event

commercialization The act of reorganizing or reworking something in order to extract profit from it

descendant One who comes from a specific ancestor

Eastern Orthodox Church The group of Christian churches that includes the Greek Orthodox, Russian Orthodox, and several other churches led by patriarchs in Istanbul (Constantinople), Jerusalem, Antioch, and Alexandria.

effigy A representation of someone or something, often used for mockery

equinox Either of the two times during each year when night and day are approximately the same length of time. The spring equinox typically falls around March 21 and the autumnal equinox around September 23.

fast To abstain from eating for a set period of time, or to eat at only prescribed times of the day as directed by religious custom or law.

feast day A day when a religious celebration occurs and an intricate feast is prepared and eaten.

firsthand From the original source; experienced in person

Five Pillars of Islam The five duties Muslims must observe: declaring that there is only one God and Muhammad is his prophet, praying five times a day, giving to charity, fasting during Ramadan, and making a pilgrimage to Mecca

foundation myth A story that describes the foundation of a nation in a way that inspires its people

Gregorian calendar The calendar in use through most of the world

hedonism The belief that pleasure is the sole good in life

Hindu A follower of Hinduism, the dominant religion of India

imam A leader; a scholar of Islam; the head of a mosque

indigenous Originating in or native to a specific region; often refers to living things such as people, animals, and plants

Islam The religious faith of Muslims. Muslims believe that Allah is the only God, and Muhammad was his prophet

Judaism A religion that developed among the ancient Hebrews. Followers of Judaism believe in one God and follow specific laws written in the Torah and the Talmud, and revealed to them by Moses.

Julian calendar Is named after Julius Caesar, a military leader and dictator of ancient Rome, who introduced it in 46 B.C.E. The Julian calendar has 365 days divided into 12 months, and begins on January 1. An extra day, or leap day, is added every four years (February 29) so that the years will average out to 365.242, which is quite close to the actual 365.242199 days of Earth's orbit.

lower realm In the Asian tradition, the place where the souls end up if their actions on Earth were not good

lunar Related to the Moon

martyr A person who willingly undergoes pain or death because of a strong belief or principle

masquerade A party to which people wear masks, and sometimes costumes or disguises

millennium 1,000 years

monarch A king or queen; a ruler who inherits the throne from a parent or other relative

monotheism The belief in the supremacy of one god (and not many) that began with Judaism more than 4,000 years ago and also includes the major religions of Islam and Christianity.

mosque An Islamic house of worship

mourning The expression of sorrow for the loss of a loved one, typically involving

movable feast A religious feast day that occurs on a different day every year

Muhammad The prophet to whom God revealed the Quran, considered the final prophet of Islam

mullah A clergyman who is an expert on the Quran and Islamic religious matters

Muslim A person who follows the Islamic religion

New Testament The books of the Bible that were written after the birth of Christ

New World A term used to describe the Americas from the point of view of the Western Europeans (especially those from France, England, Portugal, and Spain) who colonized and settled what is today North and South America.

offering Donation of food or money given in the name of a deity or God

Old Testament The Christian term for the Hebrew Scriptures of the Bible, written before the birth of Christ

oral tradition Stories told aloud, rather than written, as a way to pass down history

pagan Originally, someone in ancient Europe who lived in the countryside; a person or group that does not believe in one god, but often believes in many gods that are closely connected to nature and the natural world

pageantry Spectacle, elaborate display

parody Imitation of something, exaggerated for comic effect–for example, a parody of science fiction movies.

patria Fatherland; nation; homeland

peasant People who farm land that usually belongs to someone else, such as a landowner

penance The repentance of sins, including confessing, expressing regret for having committed them, and doing something to earn forgiveness

piety A strong belief in and correspondingly fervent practice of religion

pilgrimage A journey undertaken to a specific destination, often for religious purposes

prank A mischievous or humorous trick

pre-Columbian Of or relating to the period before Christopher Columbus arrived in the Americas

procession A group of people moving together in the same direction, especially in a type of celebration

prophecy A prediction about a future event

prophet An individual who acts as the interpreter or conveyer of the will of God and spreads the word to the followers or possible followers of a religion. A prophet can also be a stirring leader or teacher of a religious group. Capitalized it refers to Muhammad.

Protestant A member of a Christian denomination that does not follow the rule of the pope in Rome and is not one of the Eastern Orthodox Churches. Protestant denominations include Anglicans (Episcopalians), Lutherans, Presbyterians, Methodists, Baptists, and many others.

Quran The holy book of Islam

rabbi A Jew who is ordained to lead a Jewish congregation; rabbis are traditionally teachers of Judaism.

reincarnation The belief in some religions that after a person or animal dies, his or her soul will be reborn in another person or animal; it literally means, "to be made flesh again." Many Indian religions such as Hinduism, Sikhism, and Jainism, believe in reincarnation.

repentance To express regret and ask forgiveness for doing something wrong or hurtful.

requiem A Mass for the souls of the dead, especially in the Catholic Church

revel To celebrate in a joyful manner; to take extreme pleasure

ritual A specific action or ceremony typically of religious significance

sacred Connected with God or religious purposes and deemed worthy of veneration and worship

sacrifice Something given up or offered in the name of God, a deity or an ancestor.

shaman A spiritual guide who a community believes has unique powers to tell the future and to heal the sick. Shamans can mediate or cooperate with spirits for a community's advantage. Cultures that practice shamanism are found all over the world still today.

Shia A Muslim sect that believes that Ali, Muhammad's son-in-law, should have succeeded Muhammad as the caliph of Islam; a common sect in Iran but worldwide encompassing only about 15 percent of Muslims

solar calendar A calendar that is based on the time it takes Earth to orbit once around the Sun

solar Related to the Sun

solilunar Relating to both the Sun and Moon

solstice Day of the year when the hours of daylight are longest or shortest. The solstices mark the changing of the seasons–when summer begins in the Northern Hemisphere (about June 22) and winter begins in the Northern Hemisphere (about December 22).

spiritual Of or relating to the human spirit or soul, or to religious belief

Sunni The largest Islamic sect, including about 85 percent of the world's Muslims

supernatural Existing outside the natural world

Talmud The document that encompasses the body of Jewish law and customs

Torah Jewish scriptures, the first five books of the Hebrew scriptures, which serve as the core of Jewish belief

veneration Honoring a god or a saint with specific practices

vigil A period in which a person stays awake to await some event

Vodou A religion rooted in traditional African beliefs that is practiced mostly in Haiti, although it is very popular in the West Indies as well. Outside of Haiti it is called *Vodun*.

Further Resources

■ Books

National Day Traditions Around the World. By Susan Kesselring. Published in 2013 by The Child's World, North Mankato, Minn. Overviews and illustrations of national holidays, independence days, and patriotic festivals from around the world.

DK Eyewitness Books: American Revolution. By Stuart Murray. Published in 2015 by Penguin Random House, New York. Discover how a few patriots battled a mighty empire–from the Boston Massacre to the birth of a new nation.

The French Revolution. By Robert Green. Published in 2015 by Referencepoint Press, San Diego. Examines the French Revolution, including the events leading up to it; the impact of major uprisings, participants, and actions; and its lasting effect on France and the world.

Women Heroes of the American Revolution: 20 Stories of Espionage, Sabotage, Defiance, and Rescue. By Susan Casey. Published in 2017 by Chicago Review Press, Chicago. Profiles 20 female figures involved with the American Revolution. While some of the names are legendary and recognizable, most are not. These ordinary girls and women accomplished amazing feats.

Mahatma Gandhi: Champion of Indian Independence. By Monique Vescia. Published in 2018 by Rosen Publishing, New York. Learn about Mahatma Gandhi's struggle for Indian independence from Great Britain and the effect of his successful peaceful resistance strategy on world history.

■ Web Sites

Address by Patrice Lumumba, first prime minister of the Congo, on June 30, 1960, Independence Day. http://sfbayview.com/2009/06/patrice-lumumba%E2%80%99s-independence-day-speech-june-30-1960/. This text of Lumumba's speech with biographical information is of value to anyone with an interest in the modern Congo.

Australia Day. http://www.australiaday.gov.au. This Web site describes the history of Australia Day and information about current celebrations.

Belgium National Day. https://visit.brussels/en/event/National-Day. A description of the festivities in Brussels, Belgium.

Canada Day. https://www.canada.ca/en/canadian-heritage/campaigns/celebrate-canada-days/canada-day.html. This is Canada's governmental Web site, a good place to learn about the holiday.

Dieciocho: Chile's Month-Long Independence. http://acelebrationofwomen.org/2010/09/chili-independence-day-a-month-long-celebration/. Read about Chile's lengthy Independence Day celebration.

Do you remember Independence Day? http://news.bbc.co.uk/2/hi/africa/4755396.stm. Africans remember their struggles for independence.

German Reunification. https://www.washingtonpost.com/news/worldviews/wp/2016/10/03/germany-reunified-26-years-ago-but-some-divisions-are-still-strong/. This article outlines some of the challenges Germany still faces after nearly 30 years of reunification.

New Zealand History Online. https://nzhistory.govt.nz/politics/treaty/waitangi-day. This Web site has a detailed history of Waitangi Day.

Uzupio … A World Apart. http://www.vilnius-life.com/vilnius/uzupio. Explores the history and attractions of the state of Uzupio.

What to Expect on August 17th. http://www.expat.or.id/info/august17th-IndonesianIndependenceDay.html. Indonesia's Independence Day in Jakarta, its capital.

Index

Picture Credits